THE LONG ROAD HOME...

a philosophical journey.

Richard McKenzie Neal

authorHOUSE®

AuthorHouse™
1663 Liberty Drive
Bloomington, IN 47403
www.authorhouse.com
Phone: 1-800-839-8640

First published by AuthorHouse 11/13/2009

ISBN: 978-1-4490-3186-2 (e)
ISBN: 978-1-4490-3184-8 (sc)
ISBN: 978-1-4490-3185-5 (hc)

Library of Congress Control Number: 2009911379

Printed in the United States of America
Bloomington, Indiana

This book is printed on acid-free paper.

Acknowledgement:

My Mother
(Linnie Bea Warren)

December 25, 1924 --- August 23, 1988

During the writing of my books I always believed that my Mother was smiling down from above and that she's proud of the man I've become. I know she lived a troubled life and, according to my uncle Milford, never felt loved. Most of this I covered in the first book (Fridays With Landon), but at a subliminal level, her spiritual essence has been woven throughout all three manuscripts. It's only now, as my lifelong journey is winding down, that I've truly come to understand the loneliness and silent desperation that accompanied my Mother during her sojourn on earth.

She married numerous times, but none stayed. I left her when I was only 17 and she would later bury her youngest (Regina Kay) at 28. She just always seemed to be alone, and even when she wasn't...she appeared to be in a counting down mode, as in waiting for the next shoe to drop.

I want her to know that I always loved her, and that I never wanted to leave...I just couldn't stay.

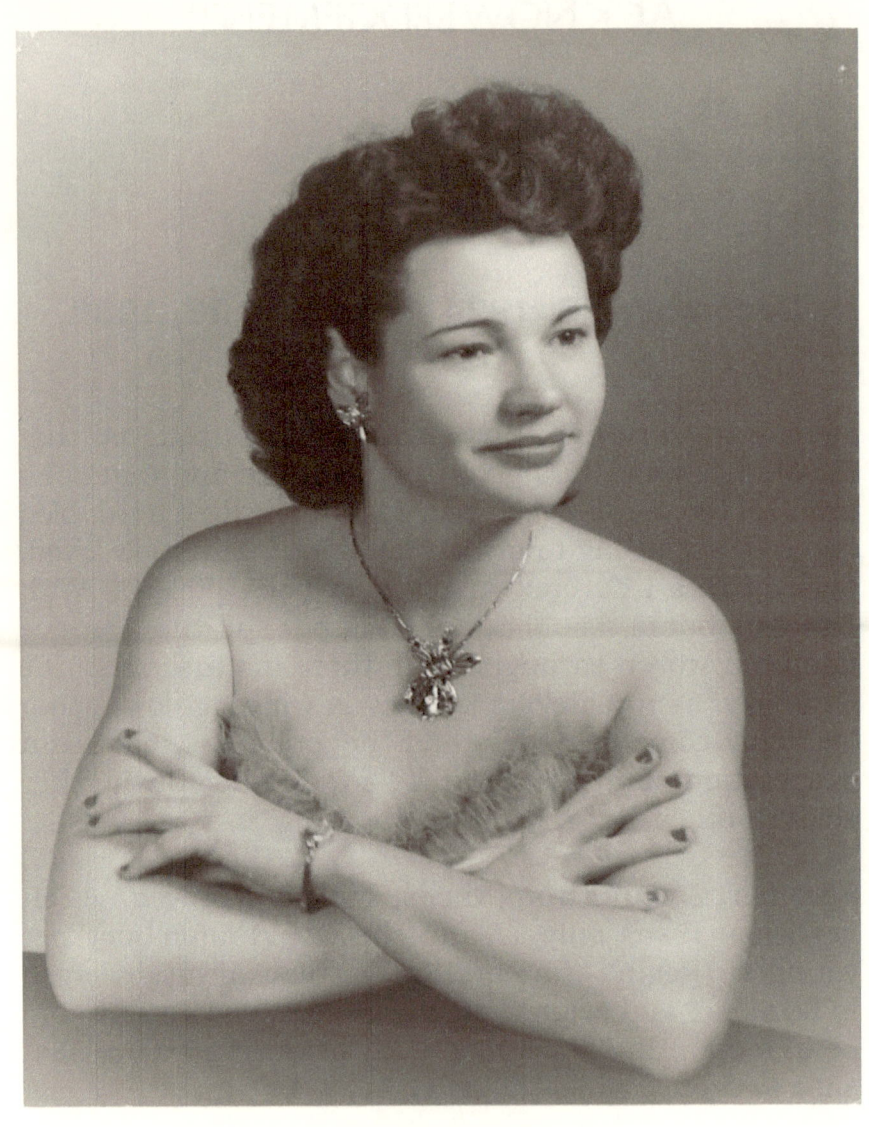

My Mother

FOREWORD

This book was precipitated by a routine road trip to my birthplace (the old country) in Arkansas. Fifty years ago I left Arkansas behind in my search for greener pastures; and except for a couple of high school reunions and the inescapable funerals, my home has been in California. The plan was a four– or five-week road trip back to the Arkansas, Texas, Oklahoma, and Louisiana areas. Driving back provided a more flexible schedule and afforded me a ground level view of the collage-like landscape that my airline flights had always denied me.

I left Orange County on a Saturday morning with *"going home"* on my mind and a list of "want to dos," "should dos," "need to dos," and "might dos." With my new GPS onboard and my philosophical roadmap in my head, I headed off into uncharted territory...even as I neglected to factor in the unknowns. In addition to an aging uncle on my mother's side and an aging aunt on my father's side, I had maintained an email relationship with a few high school friends in the area. I had loosely pre-planned numerous visits (including a very personal visit to my Mother's final resting place, at the Westmoreland Cemetery) before heading out on my discovery foray... but ended up shuffling and rescheduling as additional, unexpected opportunities opened heretofore forgotten doors into my long-buried past.

By this point in our lives (my target readers) we've all heard the old adage *"You can't go home."* But what do those words mean...to the individual? Where is home... where you were born, where you spent your childhood, where you spend your adulthood or perhaps it's a spiritual manifestation? Everyone has a different point of view.

As life winds down and the drone of existence begins to wane, I'm experiencing yet another abstract phase of my passage through this world. I feel an intangible desire or need to reach back into my past and reconnect with a by-gone time and people...living and/or dead. It feels like an elusive melody that seems distantly familiar yet conversely strange and unidentifiable. Another analogy might be that of the proverbial ghost-town tumbleweed that's being blown along helter-skelter without direction or purpose; my course *home* would also seem to be very skewed and filled with misdirection, but I feel that my path and hypothetical destination will be made clear (in time) by life's prevailing winds.

If all the above just sounds like a premonition of the inevitable (the end of life), I agree and accept that my time is ticking away. But it's not about dying...it's about *going home!* I'm not at all concerned or worrying about running out of time, but I do struggle with the concept... the reality that when my number is called, I will no longer exist. I will disappear from this world and in time, even from the minds and hearts of those who once knew me.

While I will (without bias) explore all the possibilities, I am approaching this endeavor with my own (like everyone else) thoughts and opinions. I have to wonder if the term *"going home"* isn't a misnomer and maybe... just maybe, we're trying to return to "Neverland" (*Fridays With Landon*). When we were very young we searched for that elusive, utopian community...and studies have shown that in our declining years, we slowly revert to our childhood.

Another line-of-thought is that it's all just a mirage. We already know and accept that a man can be dying of thirst, in the middle of the driest desert, and his mind will anesthetize him by creating the illusion of an oasis. If we can acknowledge that phenomenon (the mind's coping mechanism) then it shouldn't be much of a stretch to reason that elderly folks also possess those same innate coping capabilities...to ease their journey home. Of course their mirage would be about *"going home"*...not to a place, but to a kinder...more genteel time.

But of course, wouldn't all the above beg the question, "Why?" What is the driver for this (apparently) universal pilgrimage as we approach the "other" side? I have to wonder, even compare it to an addict's motivation (*The Path to Addiction*)...one more trip down that path of pleasant memories even as the host is being sacrificed.

The mind is a uniquely personal domain of thought, dreams and countless other things, like will, faith and hope. These ethereal things are as real as rocks and water...but like the mind, weightless and invisible, perhaps even timeless.

CHAPTER 1

It would seem that our early memories are, for the most part, fond recollections from our childhood and teen years. I was born in rural Arkansas where I remained until boarding that Greyhound Bus at seventeen. I never knew my father, but was aware of a couple of stepfathers and other men who were just passing through. As a family we didn't have a lot, but we didn't expect much and we never went hungry. My mother usually worked as a waitress and the stepfather that I recall being around the longest worked at an all-night gas station (6:00 PM--6:00 AM). Due to my mother's multiple marriages I grew up with a half-brother and a half-sister, but I never thought of them as anything other than my brother and sister. In retrospect I can see that I was my mother's favorite and with that same hindsight I can now see that "our" last stepfather favored my younger half-sister. My hometown was like a replication of "Pleasantville" with its righteousness and the wholesome appearance of its inhabitants; everything was black and white (no pun intended) with no shades of gray or colors. On the surface everything seemed good and as it should be, and we (the young, the naïve, the sheltered, the conditioned, the participants and everyone in-between) fell in line...because "that's just the way it was." But it wasn't Pleasantville and things weren't always good... they just festered beneath the surface and were ignored above. And the absurdity of it all was that at the end of the day, it was all just water under the bridge.

We can legislate and lobby for morality until we're blue in the face, but the greatest obstacle to making intelligent decisions is still human nature. It just seems that the more things change...the more they appear unchanged.

My farewell tour...as I jokingly referred to my road trip as, was actually an attempt at reconnecting with past friends and relatives whom I had neglected while making a life for myself in California. After explaining to my immediate family and local friends that I wasn't in any imminent danger of passing...that the trip was driven by concern for my "older" acquaintances, I headed east on my way to the South.

While this certainly wasn't my first trip back to my roots, it was different in that I was looking to revisit my past through folks who were a part of those early formative years. I can't adequately explain the change in my perspective in regard to how I saw things along those highways and byways. I noticed things that had obviously been there for decades...and longer, all part of the landscape. Even though I usually flew home on most of my necessary trips, I had driven these roads before without truly noticing the extent of trash littering the countryside. In front yards, side yards, back yards, open pastures, around businesses and even just off the shoulders of private roads. I saw everything from old washing machines to tires, old vehicles rusting away and dilapidated utility buildings in various stages of decay. But a lot of the stuff just appeared to be general everyday household trash that the resident (for whatever reason) chose to just store on the front porch or toss out on the lawn.

I'm not suggesting this trash hording is a new thing only that it never registered with me before I began this look back. I think when we're young and everything about life is new and we're bombarded by sensory overload, we don't see the trees for the forest...the debris just came with our environment. What is the driver that causes people to hold on to things that have outlived their usefulness and have no practical value? But perhaps the bigger question is...what does it have to do with *going home*? And the answer is...because it seems to be most prevalent in the same type of socioeconomic surroundings that I grew up in. It may have nothing to do with anything, but it is my past and should be investigated as part of my journey *home*.

Racism is another aspect of my rural education where perception was everything...yet had nothing to do with the truth. Growing up in Arkansas during the 40s and 50s we weren't troubled or conflicted about racism because we had no other reference point...that's just the way it was. Both sides of our little town innately understood and accepted the realities of the time...and segregation was an unspoken, self-implementing expectation of the community.

As my motoring took me through Oklahoma, Texas, Louisiana and into Arkansas, my new perspective was that the South (on the surface) had made great strides in the area of race relations. Everwhere I looked the mix appeared equal, compatible and comfortable with each other. But as I spoke with individuals from both sides

I soon learned that it's more about tolerance than the illusion of trust and respect. And my conversations also validated my longstanding quarrel with the politically correct assertion that it's only the Caucasians who are racist. The logic here is that only the ruling class majority can be racist.

My hometown (Pleasantville) was no longer my hometown. The downtown area was being abandoned with the businesses moving out to the edge of town...leaving many empty storefronts. The demographics had changed dramatically (not a condemnation, but an observation) and the old neighborhoods were run down and in various stages of disrepair. Once well-kept yards had disappeared beneath the accumulations of non-descript clutter.

Past friends and classmates were difficult to locate and often even more difficult to recognize once found. Some of course had already passed, some were in various stages of dying (cancer) and many others were in poor health requiring personal assistance, walkers, canes and vast assortments of prescription medications. Another group included men who had survived heart attacks and stroke, but would never be the same...while others were chain smokers and overweight. And yes, there were a number of folks from my age group who had managed to maintain a healthy lifestyle and they looked well. But "we" were the exception.

I also discovered that many of my cronies had never embraced or even accepted the computer as a modern-day necessity.

In addition to dissecting and examining *the long road home* for answers and possible understanding, I have a bridge that I probably should either cross or burn on my way home. Those of you who read my first book (*Fridays*

With Landon) know that I have another son out there somewhere. While we both know the other exists...we have never met. I do not know his name or where he lives, only that he is in his mid to upper 40s. He knows my name and I believe that if he really wanted to find me, he could. It's my understanding that he was adopted as a child and with that knowledge, I accept that he has a father...and it's not me.

On one hand I subscribe to the old adage that there's nothing to be gained by digging up old bones...or just let the sleeping dog lie. But perhaps on the other hand we both want to, but we're just too prideful to reach out... and having said that, I believe that pride is the chief cause of the decline in the numbers of close friends and relatives today.

CHAPTER 2

Before we get too far down this pathway I should clarify that the hording of seemingly useless objects is not an exclusive manifestation of the South. I will also be looking to separate the clinical obsessive-compulsive disorder (OCD) hoarders and collectors from the more rural, culture driven "might need it someday" mentality. For the most part, the OCD driven individuals will go unnoticed until someone from the outside sees the squalor inside their all-to-often uninhabitable home. While on the other side of the street, the culture driven folks proudly display their dirty laundry out on the lawn, or as with their outdoor comfort recliner...on the front porch, right next to the old wringer-type washing machine.

Hoarding is defined as the acquisition of, and inability to discard worthless items even though they appear (to others) to have no value. Hoarding behaviors can occur in a variety of psychiatric disorders and in the normal population, but are most commonly found in people with obsessive-compulsive disorder. The people reporting compulsive hoarding as their primary type of OCD usually experience significant distress or functional impairment from their hoarding. Those that have symptoms of indecisiveness, procrastination, and avoidance, are classified as having compulsive hoarding syndrome.

Compulsive hoarding is not just an enthusiast's passion for collecting stamps, dolls, or baseball cards. Neither is it someone who likes to "tinker" with or fix up old cars and/or broken furniture. People with compulsive hoarding syndrome may have immense difficulty throwing anything away, from the oldest paper clip, to a used food container, to an out-of-date newspaper, for fear that they might need those items in the future. Their homes are often full of stuff that the rest of us would call "junk."

The most commonly saved items include newspapers, magazines, old clothing, bags, books, mail, notes, and lists. Along with difficulties in throwing things away, compulsive hoarders have severe difficulties making decisions, perfectionism, and avoiding tasks. People with compulsive hoarding syndrome do not like to make mistakes. To prevent making a mistake, they will avoid or postpone making decisions. Even the smallest task, such as washing dishes or checking the mail may take a long time because it has to be done "right." The net result of these high standards and the fear of making a mistake is that compulsive hoarders avoid doing many tasks, because everything becomes tedious and overwhelming.

To differentiate "normal" collecting from compulsive hoarding, compulsive hoarding syndrome has been defined according to three criteria:

1. The acquisition of, and failure to discard, possessions that appear to be useless or of limited value. Compulsive hoarders have an obsessive

need to acquire and save many objects, and tremendous anxiety about discarding them... because of a perceived need for those objects and their alleged value. Sometimes an excessive emotional attachment to them will develop. A compulsive hoarder will think, "This is too good to throw away, this is important information, I might need this later on, this should not be wasted." These thoughts are generally normal, but their frequency and the importance attached to them are clearly excessive in compulsive hoarders. If they have any doubt at all as to the value of an object...no matter how trivial, compulsive hoarders will keep it...just in case.

2. Living spaces sufficiently cluttered so as to preclude activities for which those spaces were originally designed. Obviously, with many items coming into the home and very few going out, the clutter will accumulate. It does not take long for the clutter to spread onto the floors, counter tops, hallways, stairwells, garage, and cars. Beds become so cluttered that there is no room to sleep. Chairs become buried under clutter, so there is nowhere to sit. Kitchen counters become so cluttered that food cannot be prepared. For many hoarders, it gets to a point where there might be only a narrow pathway that connects each room, and the rest of the house is piled several feet high with clutter. It becomes impossible to use many areas of the house for their original purpose.

3. Significant distress and/or impairment in one's routine functionality is caused by their hoarding. Because of their desire for perfection, compulsive hoarders frequently take a long time to do even small chores. An inordinate amount of time may

be spent "churning"...moving items from one pile to another but never actually discarding any item nor establishing any consistent organizational system. Many compulsive hoarders have limited social interactions. The nature of their problem makes them socially isolated.

They are frequently too embarrassed by their clutter to have people come to their home, sometimes for many years. Some compulsive hoarders are able to work, but they will often comment that they are not working in a job that fully utilizes their skills or potential. They always come in early and leave late because they take much longer than other people to finish tasks.

While the OCD facet of hoarding has been studied extensively, the trashing of rural America has largely been written off to white trash culture. The general public thinks these people are just slobs or lazy, but most of the time it's actually driven by not wanting to waste things, and/or wanting to make the right decision about a thing that has become overwhelming to them...so they just keep it.

Rural America (in many areas) has, for generations, embraced a low-maintenance style of lawn management. To the out-of-towner it might appear that it's a deranged landscaper's version of a new art-deco craze with curious artifacts being haphazardly strewn about as the "not so pleasing to the eye" centerpieces. It has always been a part of our rural surroundings. It was there when I was growing up in Arkansas, but I didn't notice it because it was the norm...it was our world, our environment, our culture...that was just the way it was. Many folks (not all) just never seemed to be able to rid themselves of their useless, valueless belongings...and they were somehow able to ignore the ever-growing level of debris surrounding their residence...their life. And for whatever reason, personal pride never surfaced as a deterrent.

Studies have suggested that the hardships of the depression continue to influence many in rural America. And as with any culture, that subliminal message of survival has been perpetuated and passed along. Hoarding provides these individuals an emotional and psychological hedge between reality and their longstanding, ingrained fears of yet another depression.

Another line of thought that comes to mind is that trash... especially the bigger items and things that couldn't be disposed of by burning, was more difficult to discard in the olden days before universal trash pickup and disposal services. Perhaps that difficulty lead to a practice of setting things aside with the thought that, "I'll haul this old washing machine away later when I get that old truck out there in the yard fixed up and running." I can remember hauling our trash to some out-of-sight place down one of those obscure country roads where common household "stuff" was illegally being dumped...and that stuff was pretty much any and everything that I could get into the car or the bed of the truck. As I look back, it wasn't like an official dump or landfill...it was more like Arlo Guthrie's trash dumping experience recounted in his song "Alice's Restaurant." You know what I'm saying, first one idiot (seeing an opportunity) and then later another idiot (wanting to contribute) dumped their trash there until the site took on the appearance of the county dump. And you know what we say today, "It is what it is." Well, in looking back..."It was what it was."

After it became clear to me that I was probably going to write this book, I did...tactfully speak with a few folks regarding this subject during my southern tour. Most of them had a long list of real good reasons for retaining the many items that I viewed (but did not verbalize) as totally useless eyesores.

My favorite uncle (bless his heart) is holding on to an aging, dust covered, 30-plus year old, Ford sedan for sentimental reasons. He has also parked a Ford Explorer along the side of his industrial sized, twin-bay garage because he wasn't able to sell it for his asking price. I fully expect that it will be parked there for a very long time. Additionally, he has a large, new Ford truck, a completely restored 1931, Model-A, Ford...with a ragtop, and his wife has a nice sports car. The Model-A has only been driven a couple of times (more on that later) since he purchased it sometime ago. They also have a monster motor home in one of those industrial size bays parked along side the Model-A in the adjoining bay. While the coach has been a part of their fleet for many years, to my knowledge it has spent far more time in the bay than out on the road. But it provides my uncle with something to do; he goes out from time to time and starts up the engine and allows it run for a while to keep the battery up. But he fumigated us during his show and tell, motor start-up drill with me; the big doors were closed and he had forgotten that the coach was still idling when he called me over to the Model-A. He was cranking away even as he was assuring me that it would start...and it finally did, but it was missing and backfiring even as he was laboring to adjust the old manual type choke. Because it was now flooded, it was sputtering, shaking and expelling large volumes of gas vapors. Yep, we now had two vehicles that were spewing gas vapors into our confined space. It made me a little dizzy and sick to my stomach, but didn't seem to faze him. The remaining space inside that large structure was dedicated to a vast array of things that my uncle thinks he "might need someday." Those things range from old tires (that had been replaced because they had become unsafe) to any number of other items that had already outlived their usefulness. In almost every case, the things that were being stored were things that had been replaced because they were old and/or no longer practical or functional... and should have been resting in the county dump. I saw old toilets, sinks, an outdated microwave, car wheels, broken lamps and various junky household items; but additionally he had other things that I instinctively knew were special to him...relics to most, but keepsakes to him (including the Model-A). Those items provided him with instant recall of those long ago pleasant memories from his past. I believe that is a normal phase of his current *going home* chapter.

But on the lighter side, I felt like I had just been given a tour of Fred Sanford's place...

A couple other acquaintances rationalized that they were keeping their old cars for spare parts. So I'm thinking, you just purchased a replacement vehicle (not necessarily new, but a later model) and you're thinking you had better keep the old one. You're telling me that if, down the road, you should need parts for your new ride you could scavenge them from your old car...that worn-out, 15-year-old car that you gave up on...and so you had better keep it.

I also heard the logic that, "I'm keeping it because I'm going to fix it up someday." Well, from what I saw on my road trip through seven states...that car's probably going to be parked there for a very long time.

Both of the above lines of thought sounded almost capricious to me.

Bottom line (from my perspective) is that for the most part, it's a cultural thing that like racism...has been perpetuated and passed on from father to son. Our environment shapes us and as such, our slant on life will often mirror the influences that we encountered during our developmental years.

Pride of ownership (for these folks) doesn't play into the equation nor does how others view them. In their minds it's their private property and they have every right to store whatever crap they have or may accumulate, on their land and/or front porch. Again, it's a way of life for them...it's the norm, and has been for generations and nothing is going to change that mentality.

I am not suggesting that this is typical of rural America, only that it's out there and that it's ugly and rude, and it seems to smack of disregard for others and the general appearance of our neighborhoods and communities.

This seemingly self-anointed, sub-culture has given birth to several derogatory "ruralisms" such as "white trash" and "trailer trash." And while country white folks are almost always the targets of this endless ridicule, the truth is that reasonable facsimiles of this phenomenon can be identified (at some level) within any ethnic group.

CHAPTER 3

What is: Hick, Hillbilly, Yokel, Country Bumpkin, Cracker, Trailer Trash, White Trash and Redneck?

These are labels used to perpetuate a stereotype of a specific culture within American society. Contrary to popular belief, America is not the tolerant, classless society it claims to be. For centuries, it has steadily remained acceptable to lampoon and demean the culture of the rural, working-class Southerner. Even now, in the age of political correctness, it is considered tolerable and even appropriate to ridicule persons with the above distinctions... to generalize them as ignorant, unintelligent, eccentric, crude, unattractive, lazy, racist, alcoholic, religious to the point of absurdity, inbred, and prone to violent behavior. This is not to say that there are no rural Southern people possessing these characteristics. However, because it is repeatedly portrayed in literature and the media, the redneck stereotype has grown into a widespread myth that is accepted by many as universal truth.

Rural folks (poor working whites and/or white trailer trash)...not unlike urban dwellers, have their own various levels of socioeconomic divides. These differences may appear subtle to the casual observer, but when one is able to embrace the bigger picture and identify the social, cultural, economic and motivational drivers, the divide resembles the Grand Canyon.

I was born in rural Arkansas where I lived until life caused me to turn away from my roots...and move to the big city. Although I grew up outside the farm, (we lived in a small town surrounded by a sea of agriculture) I was a member of the Future Farmers of America in high school. I stomped across manure-laden pastures during those blistering hot summers when I took summer jobs picking cotton and watermelons, cutting and bailing hay and feeding the various farm animals...and I have no illusions as to the origin of beef and pork. Even though I moved away from it all at 17, rural America is still...and always has been a part of who I am.

Rural and urban Americans have different cultures, but they are not as different as many would have you believe. People should be celebrating this diversity, but all too many would use it as a wedge to divide us.

Rural Americans are neither smarter nor dumber than urban Americans. Intelligence is not a trait determined by where you were born. Intelligence is distributed evenly along a bell curve based on genetics. The intellectual elite should know better than to resort to the Lamarckian theory (A theory of biological evolution holding that acquired traits can be inherited.) when they have consistently consigned rural America to a permanent Neanderthal status.

Farming is not an occupation for the stupid. Neither is ranching nor dairying. More mathematics is required for one day of farming than an entire career of literary criticism. The urbanite might joke about their "pointy headed boss," but a rancher is his own boss with his own business who can't afford the luxury of the "Peter Principle." Most dairies are more networked than urban law offices.

Modern day experience with white trash stereotypes is, as with most modern cultural phenomenon, disseminated through movies and television. The images society has created fall into two conflicting categories. Most often the working class white is a whisky-drinking, abusive, violently racist, uneducated, macho, close-minded, dirty, fat, insensitive, monster-truck show watching, hunter who is better laughed at than associated with. Yet in rare instances, one encounters the poor white as honest, hard working, honorable, simple, loyal, God-fearing and patriotic. And there exists the dichotomy of white trash versus good country folk.

It is true that rural America is more religious than urban America. But this is only an evil to the leftists, who have replaced traditional American religious tolerance with the doctrine of exclusionary secularism. The absence of religion in all aspects of other people's daily lives is seen as social progress. The left will allow you to be religious so long as you do not elevate your god higher than the god of the secular state. Thus we see the frequency of liberal Catholic politicians who proudly proclaim that their deeply held beliefs have no power over their everyday life.

I can still recall growing up in my hometown...and that there were numerous churches, but there were no snake handlers or fire walkers. There was no religious strife at school...and the Pledge of Allegiance was recited without fear of offending someone. But today, urban America seems quite irreligious. Its not that there's necessarily fewer people of faith here, it's that the people appear to be too busy hustling to and fro, making money, to stop for a few hours to give thanks for it all.

American society has used the working class white to alternately allay their fear of faltering morality or to bolster their confidence in the correctness of the modern lifestyle. Examples of this tendency occur in the typecasting of working class whites in television series as well as films. Stemming from the disillusionment of Vietnam, Watergate and other corruptions of the time, we can trace a movement of "good country folk" in the television shows of the seventies. Programs like "The Andy Griffith Show" and "The Waltons" provided a simple, honest way of life that appealed to viewers as an escape from the cynicism and the loss of moral absolutes that was becoming prevalent in society. Once again, America turned to the South as the appropriate setting for such nostalgia.

At around the same time, we also had popular Southern sitcoms like "The Dukes of Hazzard" and "The Beverly Hillbillies," playing on the more typical stereotype of uneducated, criminal (Duke Brothers' constant battles with the corrupt Boss Hogg) characters with sub-standard eating habits and speech patterns. We also found sexy, yet innocent, women (Daisy and Ellie May) being protected by their families. The Beverly Hillbillies proved that even when poor whites stumble upon money, they retain their low class ways, and are useful only for the purposes of humor. The Dukes of Hazzard gives a solid continuation of redneck stereotypes, tempered with the idea that the Dukes are "never meanin' no harm" as the theme song implies.

The use of violence in film and writing is often a hallmark of social passion. During the 1930s there was a movement to expose the brutality of the lives of working class whites. Yet often the attempts to give aid were actually forms of condescension and control. That is commonly the effect of the literature and case studies of the time. John Ford's film adaptation of "The Grapes of Wrath" is the strongest example of the media's portrayal of dignified, poor whites. Henry Fonda and Jane Darwell, echoing the themes of Southern agrarianism (the movement for equitable distribution of land), are rural saints attacked by the forces of modern, capitalistic society.

In recent years, the popularity of poor white imagery has come in two forms. One is the simple, idiotic portrayal in the humorous sketches of Jeff Foxworthy (a middle to upper class actor...not a redneck) and the brass unorthodoxy of Roseanne, or the dark and perverse killers in movies like "Deliverance" or "Sling Blade." Though the complex and human character in Sling Blade is much easier to accept than the sodomizing mountain man in "Deliverance," both characters portray a warped sense of morality that is equated to their Southern, poor white upbringing. The father of the killer in Sling Blade is shown surrounded by religious iconography and he and his wife blatantly use religion to justify their horrific treatment of the child and the murder of an unwanted baby that is born to them. The depth of ignorance necessary to explain the character's behavior is only fitting in the environment of the poor white. Filled with domestic violence and dark secrets, the Southern small town setting ensures that such events would not take place in any other context.

Deliverance may be the most well known and damaging film centered around poor whites, in this case "hillbillies." Deliverance embodies all the fears of modern, urban America concerning what is most primitive and dangerous in the character of man. The conflict is between modern mainstream capitalist America and the lurking potential for evil in mankind; an evil that has been left behind in our progressive, evolving culture, but lingers in those uneducated, inbred mountaineers still dwelling within their own remote and ignorant society. In the film urban, macho men take-on the raw brutality of nature and its inhabitants with no respect and pay the price. The punishment is one of male on male rape by the embodiment of poor white trash, confirming mainstream America's fear of the poverty stricken savage.

The view from inside the working class is much more complex. The working class white is operating off its own cultural, family and individual biases; yet coupled with these are the pervasive, historically assumed ideas that violence, racism and fundamentalism are somehow inherent in its class. Even if one becomes aware of the layers of identification applied to oneself, and most people do not, a battle against your own heritage is difficult at best, and usually impossible. The class, to which we are born, where our family circulates and our formative years are spent, is the guiding principle with which we view other groups and their cultural beliefs within our life experience.

Films that show poor whites as violent people who attack wealthy citified whites allow the rich to justify their treatment of "white trash" by portraying the poor whites as racist, criminal and uneducated. This allows other typically marginalized groups to join upper class whites against the white trash. This justifies upper class stereotyping of poor whites and serves to aid in relieving upper class white guilt over treatment of "others" in the past.

The hatred and condescension of the poor seems to be the last available method of prejudice in our society. Just as Americans have made an effort to educate, understand and alter the treatment of marginalized groups and alternate cultures within our society, we have held on to poor whites as a group to demean. Making assumptions about groups of any sort on societal and biased definitions is flawed in any situation. As with other groups there must be an effort taken to use an open mind and individual code to ascribe merit to those in our world.

These generalizations are inaccurate myths because they do not acknowledge the intricacies of a culture. Every cultural group exhibits positive and negative characteristics that form its identity, and every individual belonging to that group is unique. It is socially permissible to over-generalize and discriminate against the "redneck" culture because its main distinction... aversion to progress...excludes it from the mainstream. America has become a nation obsessed with the notion of progress at all costs. Rural, working class, Southern culture, with its moral absolutes, local allegiances, and strong familial bonds is by nature resistant to progress. Their unwillingness to adapt to the changing norms of modem and postmortem society has made rednecks the subjects of persecution.

Unlike other persecuted groups, most rural working class Southerners have made no attempt to fight the attacks on their culture. This may be the result of a laid-back, easy-going manner. Perhaps many are unaware that the ridicule and contempt of their assumed and/or fabricated traits could result in the total destruction of their true culture...and consequently the abandonment of the actual merits it possesses. Many of these old-fashion principles...including forthrightness, chivalry, hospitality, and devoutness are unique and valuable. Rural Southerners need to realize they are worth defending. Perhaps the question the rest of America needs to ask itself is: Have we reached the point where anything timeless is considered backward?

CHAPTER 4

Racism in the United States has been a major issue since the colonial era. Historically, the country has been dominated by a settler society of religiously and ethnically diverse Whites. The heaviest burdens of racism in the country have historically fallen upon Native Americans, Asian Americans, African Americans, Latin Americans, Irish Americans and some other immigrant groups and their descendants. White Americans are by no means exempt from discrimination themselves, but it is significantly less common.

Major racially structured institutions include slavery, Indian reservations, segregation, residential schools (for Native Americans), internment camps, and affirmative action. Racial stratification has occurred in employment, housing, education and government. Formal racial discrimination was largely banned in the mid-20th century, and it came to be perceived as socially unacceptable and/or morally repugnant as well, yet racial politics remain a major phenomenon.

One of the issues I want to address here is the supposition linking slavery to racism. The misrepresentation here is that only Blacks were slaves and thus have some special right to a "pity party" because their ancestors were slaves, and that anyone who owned slaves was a racist. This is not true...

The word "slave" is a transliteration of the Greek word *slavos*, which rightly applies only to White European Slavs from the countries of Yugoslavia, Czechoslovakia, Slavonia, Russia, Poland, Hungary, and others. The Slavonic tribes are the roots of all European White people. For a thousand years, so many millions of these White European Slavs were captured and sold as servants, that the word slaves became universally used for the word "servant" and was only later applied to Black servants. Every White person in America has ancestors who were slaves, including the Scots, British, French, and Germans. In the early colonies of America, Whites were regularly sold as permanent slaves. If it were justifiable, Whites would be much more justified in having a "chip on their shoulder" or a pity party because more of their ancestors were slaves and for a longer period of time. Almost all Blacks in the United States were under slavery for less than 100 years. Furthermore, only five percent of all Black slaves shipped by Black masters out of Africa ever came to the United States. Most Black slaves were shipped to South America or the West Indies.

The White European Slavs, or slaves, were sold to Romans, Arabs, Germans, and even to Black African masters in northern Africa, particularly Egypt, Libya, and Ethiopia. Were these Black masters in Africa racists because they owned White European slaves? If not, then neither can they call Southerners like George Washington, Thomas Jefferson, and Jefferson Davis racists because they owned slaves. What hypocrisy and bigotry to criticize only White Southerners or the Confederate States for owning slaves. Nearly every nation in the world owned slaves, especially the Black masters in Nigeria, where most American Blacks have their roots. Accordingly, if flags of nations that owned slaves are to be labeled as racist, then nearly all the flags in the world are racist, especially the African flag of Nigeria which dealt so overwhelmingly in the slave trade.

To say that slaves were mistreated in the Old South is to say that the most Christian group of people in the entire world, the so-called "Bible Belt," mistreated their servants and violated the commandments of Jesus their Lord. Just the opposite was true. In the Old South there were numerous laws that protected servants from abuse, just as there are laws today that protect wives or children from abuse. But just because a few men abuse their wives and children does not make marriage or having children a cruel and hateful endeavor. The same is true for slavery. Of course, there were masters who violated the law and mistreated their servants, such as Union General William T. Sherman, who owned a number of slaves before the War and who was constantly in court facing charges for abusing them. That is what the laws were for, to stop Yankees like Sherman from mistreating their slaves. The incidence of abuse, rape, broken homes, and murder are one hundred times greater today in the housing projects than they ever were on the slave plantations in the Old South.

The truth is, that nowhere on the face of the earth, in all of history, were servants better treated or better loved than they were in the Old South by White, Black, Hispanic, and Indian slave owners. Yes, even Native American Indians owned slaves in the Old South. While seven percent of Southern Whites owned slaves, two percent of free Blacks in the South also owned slaves. For example, in 1860, the U.S. Census Bureau reported that around 10,000 free Blacks owned some 60,000 Black slaves. It was a Black slave master, named Anthony Johnson, who sued and won his case in a Virginia court in 1653 that changed temporary servitude into lifetime servitude. Thus, this Black slave owner established permanent slavery in Virginia.

When the U.S. Government relocated the Cherokee Indians, nearly 30 percent of the people moving along the "Trail of Tears" out West...were Black slaves belonging to the Cherokees. Just as White European slaves were primitive, barbaric pagans who practiced human sacrifice, incest, witchcraft, and idolatry, yet when converted to Christianity, learned trades and skills and became a civilized people under Black, Oriental, and White masters, so also did Black African barbaric pagans become civilized Christians with skills and trades under slavery in the Old South.

Slavery was a family institution in the Old South. A typical family plantation had one family of Whites living next door to one family of Blacks. They had the same last name, worked in the same fields side by side, played together, prayed together, raised each other's children, took care of each other in sickness, and all in all, loved one another, just like family. It was at these small family farms that Southern Blacks were taught about and converted to Christianity by the millions. It is also true that those converted Black Southerners are grateful today for those teachings, just as our White European ancestors are grateful for their conversion to Christianity while slaves to Black masters in northern Africa, such as the Black Coptic Christians in Egypt, one of the oldest Christian groups in the world. Remember, it was not from Yankees that the Southern Blacks learned about Jesus Christ; for the most part, it was from Southern slave owners.

It was there, on those family plantations, that Blacks learned trades and skills such as farming, saw milling, carpentry, and even driving steamboats and railroad trains. Even the Abolitionist Yankee government's Department of Education admitted in 1892, after the total failure of the "Reconstruction Experiment," that the best technical education that the world had ever seen, was the education that was given to the slaves by their masters before their emancipation.

It should also be remembered that the Blacks from Nigeria, the most populous region in Africa, were not civilized and not Christian, practicing voodoo, cannibalism, and witchcraft, just as the White Europeans did. Other Blacks in Nigeria captured these Blacks in tribal wars. White people did not run through the jungles of Africa kidnapping Blacks and making them slaves. Black Africans captured and sold other Blacks as slaves; they were already slaves before they ever set foot on a Spanish, Portuguese, English, or New England Yankee slave ship. Such ships stayed anchored off shore for fear of jungle diseases and the slaves were rowed out in long boats by Africans and put on board. Many of these slaves were already riddled with disease and half-starved.

All slave ships from the United States sailed from the Northern states of Massachusetts, Rhode Island, New York, New Jersey, and Delaware under the United States flag. Not one Southern ship sailed to Africa to bring back slaves. This slave trading was the big business of the rich New England Yankees. They traded rum made in Northern factories to Black African slave owners for their slaves and then traded most of the slaves to South America or the West Indies for molasses, and then manufactured the molasses into rum and made another trip. Only five percent of the African slaves ever reached the United States, and with rare exception, the life of a slave in the United States was ten times better than his life had been as a slave in Africa.

A war over slavery...not hardly! The Confederate States of America even offered to free all Southern slaves in return for independence; Lincoln refused the offer. The term "free state" meant free from Blacks. Northerners did not want to live with Blacks, slave or free, and many Northern states and territories actually passed laws prohibiting free Blacks from entering into them. Lincoln himself stated the opinion of the Northern people during a meeting with a group of Black leaders during the War, saying, "There's an unwillingness on the part of our people (Northern Whites) to live with you free colored people. Whether this is right or wrong, I am not prepared to discuss, but it is a fact with which we must deal. Therefore, I think it best for us to separate." Acting upon this sentiment, Abraham Lincoln and the United States Congress purchased land, passed laws, and started shipping free Northern Blacks out of the country down to poverty-stricken Haiti. Lincoln put together several such schemes to remove free Blacks from the United States, to send some back to Africa and some to Central and South America. At the end of the War, a few weeks before Lincoln was assassinated, Union General Benjamin Butler asked him what he was going to do with all the recently free Southern Blacks. To this Lincoln replied, "I think we should deport them all."

Meanwhile, down South, Confederate States President Jefferson Davis and his wife Varina were adopting an eight-year-old free Black orphan boy named Jim Limber. After his mother died, little Jim was placed with a free Black family as foster parents. However, this family badly mistreated him to such a degree that the news reached the ears of the President and Mrs. Davis, who, in the middle of the War, took the time and effort to intercede and rescue Jim from this child abuse. Little Jim's wounds were doctored and he was welcomed into the Confederate White House as a member of the Davis family. President Davis himself went to court in Richmond and had free papers registered on Jim Limber, so he would always be free. Even when our President was on his way to prison for trying to obtain independence and self-government for the Southern people, he made arrangements and provided for Jim Limber's future education and care. In the Old South it was not uncommon for Blacks to take in orphaned Whites or for Whites to take in orphaned Blacks. There was a relationship between Blacks and Whites that Northerners even today do not understand or appreciate.

Additionally, racism that had been viewed primarily as a problem in the Southern states, burst onto the national consciousness following the Great Migration. The relocation of millions of African Americans from their roots in the Southern states to the industrial centers of the North after World War I, particularly in cities such as Boston, Chicago, and New York (Harlem). In these northern cities racial tensions exploded most violently in Chicago where lynching and mob-directed hangings, usually racially motivated...increased dramatically in the 1920s.

The Pacific and Western states were often portrayed to those on the East Coast as more liberal in terms of race relations in the 1960s and 1970s, but California legally allowed racial segregation of public facilities until the 1950s and other forms of racism were felt there as well.

Racist attitudes, or prejudice, are still held by moderate portions of the U.S population. Members of every American ethnic group have perceived racism in their dealings with other groups. And perceived or otherwise, allegations of racism have become a social tool in today's politically correct world.

The South, the Confederate history, and by extension, the Confederate battle flag, have suffered for many years from the relentless hatchet job of false propaganda heaped upon them by the news media, the education system, and, of course, Hollywood and television. It appears that they wish to drive a wedge between Southern Blacks and Whites, much as the carpetbaggers did after the War for Southern Independence and much as the Northern news media drove a wedge between the North and South before the War. It is important to remember that movies such as Roots and North and South are make-believe, fiction. In other words, they are not totally true, just like Uncle Tom's Cabin, written before the War, was not true. One must wonder if the only reason such false propaganda is produced and promoted by the movie and television industry, is to make Blacks hate Whites, especially Southern Whites.

For example, the Confederate battle flag has no more to do with the Ku Klux Klan than the Christian cross, which the Klan carries and burns or the flag of the United States that the Klan says the Pledge of Allegiance to...yet the news media and Hollywood constantly try to connect the Confederate flag to the Klan in their propaganda. However, the news media never ask preachers if they are Klan members, because they wear a cross around their necks or link the American Legion to the Klan because they carry the U.S. flag. It is time to put an end to this anti-Confederate bigotry. It is past time that the truth was told. Hitler's tactic of "tell a big enough lie often enough and people will believe it" has been utilized to the fullest extent, to smear the Confederate States of America and its symbols such as the battle flag.

The Confederate battle flag represents all Southerners and even Northern Confederates from states such as Ohio, Illinois, Indiana, and others, who supported the

South and who even tried to secede from the Union and form their own nation but whose efforts for freedom were crushed by Lincoln's troops. Confederate Indians, Hispanics, Blacks, and Whites all received Confederate pensions after the War and attended Confederate veterans' reunions together, year after year, just as they had suffered and fought together during the War. The Confederate battle flag represents all Confederates, regardless of race or religion, and is the symbol of less government, less taxes, and the right of a people to govern themselves. It is flown in memory and honor of our Confederate ancestors and veterans who willingly shed their blood for Southern independence.

Fortunately, most people have not been deceived by such hate-mongering tactics, as is evidenced in a recent Louis Harris poll which shows that 92 percent of the Southern people, of all races, are not offended by the Confederate battle flag, and that 68 percent of Blacks nationwide are not offended. Unfortunately, a few too many have believed the lies about the Confederate battle flag, which has resulted in unjustified and horrible intolerance, bigotry, hatred, violence, and even murder.

I'm guessing this all sounds like a public defender's closing argument for his defenseless, indigent client who, without credible character references, must rely on the truth. And of course we already know that the supply of truth always greatly exceeds its demand.

If I'm truly trying (philosophically) to return home, it must be a transparent passage without blinders or preconceived niceties.

CHAPTER 5

I realize of course that progress is inevitable, and that it's one of the natural branches on our evolutionary tree...but at what cost? It can be said that during every generation the elders were preaching the same gloom and doom; that the young were out of control and taking them all to Hell in a hand basket. I accept that because I heard it myself growing up in Arkansas, but my argument is that today's generation is moving at warp speed, on autopilot and moving into uncharted territory. As Captain Kirk would say, "Boldly going where no man has gone before." The problem with their flight is that there's no one on the flight deck with experience, insightful knowledge or any willingness to look back...they already know it all. And without a historical reference point, this is their norm and it's all good from their limited perspective. It's all about fast moving, high tech progress and if you're not on-board...then you're out-of-touch with reality. And so you ask, "What's the problem...what's the cost?"

Defining the cost will be difficult at best and impossible in many areas given the abstract nature of our forfeitures. These losses, for the most part, can't be measured in dollars or tangible material things. And because it's the intangibles that are becoming extinct, too many in today's accelerated, "me" lifestyle are oblivious to what's slipping away from us as a society. The two biggies that immediately come to mind are "common-sense" and "common-courtesies."

Although the phrase common sense is used reflexively without any real consideration of its etymology, it is the expression of common, generally held, customs, traditions and manners, the backbone of society.

In this society, common sense refers to conduct grounded in sound judgment, free of emotion and ideological passion. The salutary effects of a thought process rooted in the national patrimony makes common sense a basic tenet of American life. To the extent common sense is in short supply, the bonds to the past are being loosened, if not severed.

An attachment to common sense is like belief in common law...the unwritten, customary norms that evolve over centuries; the countervailing force against political and social convulsions, the balance wheel in society.

For most of American history political ideas were evaluated on a common sense barometer. However lofty the ideas, they were invariably tested against the common sense standard. It is, therefore, not surprising that common sense has served as a magnificent bulwark against revolution and, until very recently, revolutionary zeal of the kind that periodically afflicts France has not been a factor in American politics.

In thinking about the future it is imperative that common sense embodying the national tradition be retained as a guidepost for generations to come. If the cultural continuum is interrupted, society pays dearly in the form of moral confusion. Common sense is an instrument for preserving and promoting the moral principles on which the nation is founded. But it is not a goal in its own right.

Common sense is the north star of social intercourse; it is not however, the constellation of stars that comprise moral sentiment and religious tradition. Common sense is a necessary but not sufficient condition for social order, a point made by George Washington in his Farewell Address.

A danger within our democratic republic is that citizens often believe that freedom of choice can be interpreted as complete freedom of action, that any act not condemned is thereby sanctioned. It is the combination of common sense along with moral beliefs rooted in religion that represents a counter weight to the natural temptation for expansive freedom as license.

Reason is not omniscient. The edifice of social order is built on a foundation of commonly accepted moral principles, Descartes ("I think, therefore I am.") to the contrary notwithstanding.

If one accepts that human nature tends toward evil...what further evidence from history is needed to demonstrate this premise...an emphasis on custom, accepted rules, tradition, and family are the moderating influences that create social equilibrium.

An ability to distinguish between good and evil...the hallmark of education for Thomas Jefferson, assumes an ability to apply common sense and moral judgment. But in a complex world of moral relativism and a natural inclination forever expanding freedom of expression, there is a social tension between consciousness and conscience. Mankind has the ability to make choices that can either be an opportunity for reaching new horizons or a pitfall leading to degradation.

The book of Proverbs maintains "when there is no vision, a people perish," but that vision must be framed by morality, common sense and traditional norms. National spirit may soar, but it helps if the citizen's view is planted firmly in the soil of experience, experience that is handed down from parent to child, from teacher to student as common sense.

Existentialists in our midst often fail to appreciate the experience of the past. They search in vain for a tabula rasa (virgin, un-opinionated mind) on which to imprint utopian goals. For them, history is merely a dream from which they will awaken. Fortunately for the nation, this position is restricted to universities and other warrens of received wisdom.

Common sense is being challenged today, but it is not easily expunged. Like folkways, it exists in stories told to children and the guidance offered by parents.

The United States has the capability and responsibility to preserve and transmit the moral principles that gave this new nation vitality by leading the individual and the public through the thickets of moral confusion and serving as a barrier against descent into the abyss.

This is not easily done when any restriction on free expression is resisted, but with a subtle hand, conviction in our legacy and the application of common sense, the past can be a handmaiden of an exalted future vision.

Each day we transmit a series of messages that communicate how we regard others. This is done either verbally or through other means affecting our senses. These messages can either be perceived as positive or negative. For example, someone who dresses or smells badly is sending a message that he has no regard for the others around him, as does foul habits such as belching or flatulence. Conversely, good grooming means you care how people perceive you. Other positive messages are conveyed through such things as greetings and handshakes, punctuality, and simple manners. Common courtesy, therefore, is concerned with sending positive messages as opposed to negative. It also means our ability to practice common courtesy is a reflection of our character and how we want other people to treat us.

When referencing common courtesies I'm most definitely not referring to "political correctness" which is concerned with pseudo-courtesies for political purposes. Instead, common courtesy represents a genuine respect for the human spirit and how we should interact. This is much more than just saying please and thank you, it's treating others, as we would want others to treat us.

A lot of people underestimate the importance of a handshake. Actually it is the single most important message we can convey in an introduction. Some people like to give a strong vice grip handshake in an attempt to intimidate you, but most handshakes today by young people are weak and flabby. Actually you need to find a good balance, not too flabby and not too strong. Further, look the other person square in the eyes when you shake hands, this conveys your sincerity in meeting the person. Do not trust anyone who simply shakes your hand but doesn't look you in the eyes; they simply do not care about you.

While driving, did you ever want to switch lanes, but were prevented from doing so by the heavy traffic? How did you feel when someone recognizing your problem slowed down, waved to you, and let you in? Your mounting frustration was instantly transformed into relief and thankfulness, wasn't it?

Later, when you saw someone else in a similar jam didn't you also slow down and let him or her in? You were sharing and spreading the kindness you received from another. How do you suppose the driver you just helped will act? Most likely, they will do likewise. Look at the power we have to sweeten the lives of others! "The power of one!" Sometimes, the seemingly trivial acts we perform are the most important.

Courtesy is an example. We may refer to it in different ways, such as civility, good manners, good behavior, good conduct, politeness, decency, respect for others, thoughtfulness, kindness, and consideration. No matter what we call it, courtesy is not trivial.

Manners are of more importance than laws. Manners are what vex or soothe, corrupt or purify, exalt or debase, barbarize or refine us, by a constant, steady, uniform, insensible operation, like that of the air we breathe in.

Are those words too strong? Not at all...think about it. Would a considerate person steal, a kind student bully, a thoughtful person cheat or a respectful person murder, probably not. Manners and morals flow from the same principles...and that's a consideration for others. So, as we raise the level of courtesy that is practiced in our society, we can lower our crime rate. We tend to think today that those good manners and high morals are entirely separate. But the truth is, they are a continuum. Bad manners and soaring crime rates are all part of the same disease.

Unfortunately, TV, movies, the media and merchandisers often portray rudeness and aggressiveness as being "in." Not wanting to be left out and wishing to be "cool," the young blindly follow the examples espoused by their heroes and heroines. Who can blame them? They don't know any better. They have yet to learn that rudeness is the imitation of strength practiced by the weak. They don't understand that polite people are enamored with life while those who are rude are bitter. Our manners, then, are the clothes we wear. It reveals what type of person we are. We need to teach the young by our examples that the strong are kind. The strong reach out and connect with others. They unite, uplift, and improve the world. Those who act kindly ennoble life because they imitate God.

Character used to matter, but today it seems that it's personality and appeal that matter. Personality and appeal are like a loose-fitting cloak that hides the flaws and imperfections of the wearer. For a time, a cloak can make what is unappealing look quite presentable. In contrast, character reveals the depths of a person's heart and mind. It guides the person even in the hidden moments of life that no one else can see.

CHAPTER 6

The Alice in Wonderland restructuring of our ever-changing world (my out-of-touch perspective) seems to be a place where up is down, left is right and day is night.

The consequences of marriage affect every aspect of our society. It encompasses the most intimate elements of personal privacy and personal love and reaches the pillars of the sacred institutions of a culture. Marriage is the pillar of society, but it is also the pillar of government, business, and even the military. Marriage cuts to the very heart of a nation. As goes marriage...so goes the nation. It infiltrates every facet of human life...not only for the married but also for the unmarried. When marriages prosper, the nation rises; when marriages fail, the nation falls. Divorce not only rattles the foundation of the judicial system and psychiatry, but also through its influence on the children, alters the course of the next generation. Divorces are the steps to the grave of a culture and a nation. The study of culture, corporate or private, is the study of marriage.

The latest figures on out-of-wedlock births should be setting off alarm bells in every corner of the country. After a number of years at the wholly unacceptable level of one of every three births out-of-wedlock, the numbers in the last three years have lunged to 40 percent. This is a crisis that is direr than our floundering economy, and more dangerous than our foreign enemies. America cannot remain a superpower abroad with a crumbling family structure at home.

The crisis these new numbers represent is a crisis in male-female commitment. We are facing increasing gender rejection. Something is deeply and dangerously wrong between the sexes. Young American men are increasingly unable to commit to the mothers of their children.

In 1965, Daniel Patrick Moynihan saw a 24 percent out-of-wedlock birthrate in the black community and sounded the alarm. All the great gains of the civil rights movement were threatened by the breakdown of the black family, Moynihan warned. He then suffered the fate of the prophet without honor. As the messenger bearing the bad news, he was very nearly stoned. His unheeded warnings about crime, drugs, and educational failures have become the collection of pathologies that all Americans now know all too well. Today, Moynihan's distinguished public career is honored, but his message was/is too little heeded.

What is driving these menacing numbers? Why are 40 percent of American children being deprived at birth of their fathers? By the time they reach age 18, fully 60 percent of young Americans have seen their mothers and fathers break up. This comes either from divorce or from the breakup of cohabiting relationships. Or it stems from never-formed families. How can the young learn commitment if their parents remain uncommitted?

This lunge toward a 40 percent out-of-wedlock birthrate is the sign of a culture unraveling. In its wake will come a blighted future of increasing crime, educational failures, drugs, and poverty. It is not poverty that is driving these numbers; the out-of-wedlock birthrate is driving poverty.

What can be done? First, do no harm...or do no more harm. We must recognize that federal family planning efforts have contributed to this crisis. All data shows that young people who have multiple sex partners are less likely to marry and, if married, are less likely to remain married. Why then should our tax dollars subsidize a "hook up" culture?

We are shoveling money at groups whose sole purpose is to facilitate out-of-wedlock sexual activity.

Second, we must recognize that religious attendance is positively correlated with marriage, family formation, and family stability.

I, of course, remember wearing my 501 Levis down around my hips during the '50s...but my underwear wasn't being flaunted as a part of my ensemble; and I wasn't constantly preoccupied with the continuous task of manually maintaining the desired line of demarcation.

But today (and you know where I'm going) bad grammar, spelling and syntax seem to perfectly fit the individuals who wear baggy pants that expose their underwear, ass, pubic hair or whatever. I am not sure that local bans against such questionable fashion statements are the solution or could even be enforced, but I am pretty sure that not so long ago the wearers would have been arrested for indecent exposure. I rather doubt that a person, who has to pull up his pants every five steps or so in order to prevent them from gathering around his ankles, can be a very productive member of society.

And let's not forget that the saggy pants fashion originated in prisons...not as a choice though, but a necessity. While sagging did start in prison, it resulted from the fact that many of the clothes given to the inmates were too large. But belts weren't allowed because of the potential for suicide attempts and/or their possible use as a weapon if an inmate had one. The style was then adopted by some rap stars and the hip-hop industry, then migrated to other music genres and has since become the fad for teens of all ethnicities.

But make no mistake, most parents and the general public views the baggy pants as degrading eyesores. And the kids will tell you that they know how much it bugs their parents, and that's part of the reason they insist on dressing as they do. With that knowledge, I have to ask, "Why would the parents purchase these ridicules garments for their son(s) in the first place?" Well, do you remember the movie "Children of The Corn?" That's the only logical explanation I can come up with for such an illogical, parental determination in regard to their child's mature, social development. But we know the real answer...in today's world, more often than not, the parents are just puppets and the children are the puppeteers.

The clothes we wear are never just clothes; they always make a statement...send a message. We, the general public should be appalled by the message those saggy pants guys are sending...I am.

We have intentionally "dumbed" down our schools, ignored our history, and no longer teach our founding documents, why we are exceptional, and why we are worth preserving. Students by and large cannot write, think critically, read, or articulate. Parents are not revolting, teachers are not picketing, and school boards continue to back mediocrity.

In speaking with a teacher friend of mine recently, I learned that continuation schools often have afternoon only classes for individuals who don't do well in the regular morning sessions. These are kids who were transferred to a continuation school because they couldn't adapt to a standard classroom environment and/or get along with others. The routine and structure of the classes at their local schools just didn't work for them...they couldn't progress.

Most at continuation schools are able to get it together and handle a near-normal academic schedule. But many just can't seem to get going before noon, they are tired and sleepy...unfocused and irritable. Since these students and their parents aren't willing to make the necessary adjustments in their lifestyle...our schools, always looking to appease the public, made the arbitrary alterations. Afternoon classes have been put in place for those individuals who routinely spend most of their nights texting and/or playing their video games. And again, we seem to have a reversal of roles here...the parents (puppets) and the children (puppeteers).

Our graduates are leaving college and merging into the "real world" armed with Double Majors in "Western Civilization Bad Mouthing"...and reading and writing at the Fourth Grade level.

Unfortunately, these are tomorrow's voters and leaders and they are ill equipped to deal with the realities of the real world. They truly seem to believe that world peace is now on the horizon...if we'll just keep apologizing to the religious fanatics from around the globe. If we'll sit down together and seek to understand "their culture"... and just get to know each other. You know...just like Rodney King once asked, "Can't we all just get along?" Well, in this case, based on the history of mankind...it doesn't look good.

The history of mankind is yesterday's news for this "now" generation and not a relevant barometer in assessing today's escalating, religious conviction driven carnage. It matters not that man has fought this battle for centuries; from the perspective of the young and naïve, the end is in sight (the end may well be in sight, but not the end of man's injustice to man).

We are at war with an enemy we cannot name for fear of offending people of the same religion who cannot wait to slit the throats of your children if they have the opportunity to do so. Yes, it's all with the best of intentions...but of course, the road to Hell is paved with good intentions.

No people in history have ever survived, who thought they could protect their freedom by making themselves inoffensive to their enemies.

We have now established the precedent of protesting every close election...even violently in California over a proposition that is so controversial that it wants marriage to remain between one man and one woman. Did you ever think such a thing possible just a decade ago? I'm not coming down on either side of this fence, just comparing yesteryear with today...progress, I'm told.

We have corrupted our sacred political process by allowing un-elected judges to write laws that radically change our way of life, and even allow mainstream Marxist groups like ACORN and others to turn our voting system into a banana republic.

Over time we all leave our footprints in the shifting sands of time, the only question is...will we lead or be led?

CHAPTER 7

Responsibility, accountability, and consequences... remember those words? Yes, words that used to mean something, but today they're just window dressing. We have become a society of the blameless...and always quick to point a finger.

And then there's the ever-present opportunist looking to work our court system, through lawsuits, to subsidize his extravagant lifestyle. People today seem to sue at the drop of a hat...in part, because our courts have become so liberal that everyone wants to get in on the action. Frivolous becomes a very subjective word once the gavel goes down inside the courtroom.

My schoolteacher friend also spoke about the inordinate amount of time spent by teachers and administrators documenting and defending routine district policies when reprimanding problem students. The parents (in too many cases) try to place the blame at the wrong doorsteps; any doorsteps except theirs...the problem couldn't possibly reside at their residence. By refusing to take responsibility these parents are, through the process of osmosis, teaching their children that accountability can be avoided and consequences negated. And this not only plays out at school but in everyday living...parents all to often, automatically become defensive when confronted with issues of accountability regarding their children... and at whatever age. They just don't want to hear about it because their children are clones of themselves.

Responsibility assumption is a doctrine in the personal growth field holding that each individual has substantial or total responsibility for the events and circumstances that befall them in their life. While there is little that is notable about the notion that each person has at least some role in shaping their experience, the doctrine of responsibility assumption posits that the individual's mental contribution to his or her own experience is substantially greater than is normally thought. "I must have wanted this" is the type of catchphrase used by adherents of this doctrine when encountering situations, pleasant or unpleasant, to remind them that their own desires and choices led to the present outcome.

The term responsibility assumption thus has a specialized meaning beyond the general concept of taking responsibility for something, and is not to be confused with the general notion of making an assumption that a concept such as "responsibility" exists.

Accountability is a concept in ethics with several meanings. It is often used synonymously with such concepts as responsibility, answerability, enforcement, blameworthiness, liability and other terms associated with the expectation of account giving. As an aspect of governance, it has been central to discussions related to problems in both the public and private worlds.

Accountability is defined as "A is accountable to B when A is obliged to inform B about A's (past or future) actions and decisions, to justify them, and to suffer punishment in the case of misconduct."

Consequence is the concept of a resulting effect (cause and effect), arising from another action. In general terms, it is used to indicate that all human actions, particularly crime, sin, and even just generally misbehaving will/can produce profound effects.

The three previously defined words "should" be the governing, building blocks of life for the individual, the family, the community, and beyond. But the concept seems to be languishing in our past...

The irresponsible come at us from all directions and in all shapes, sizes and colors...but they all share one commonality. They're seeking to blame someone else for their failures and thereby avoiding responsibility, accountability, and the inevitable consequences that naturally follow. Many times a lawsuit is necessary to facilitate this avoidance of responsibility. And then, of course, if someone else can be held responsible...then that someone, by default, becomes the party of accountability and as such must suffer the consequences...as in a monetary settlement.

Errors in judgment will be made...but others can be blamed.

So why are the numbers of lawsuits increasing? I will suggest several factors, but the leading drivers are the increasing number of lawyers and the rise in the numbers of class action lawsuits in the 1970s. Those class action suits provided the large trial firms with hefty war chests to elect legislators friendly to their causes. Other causal triggers may be that today's population is using an increasing number of products whose innards are a complete mystery to them, better communication (which make it easier for people to realize they have an actionable case), and easier for lawyers to collect clients... because of our cultural shift which has convinced parents that if their baby drowns in a bucket, the bucket's manufacturer is somehow at fault for failing to warn them that this could happen.

But the single biggest factor, I would argue, is that we're getting richer. That means that we drive more miles and consume more goods, which of course increases the chances of one of our toys somehow going wrong. It also gives us more income out of which to pay for lawyers, and makes more companies look attractive as targets for those lawsuits. If lawsuits are the price we pay for getting richer, then they're a bargain that many are willing to invest in.

Getting sued by an employee is one of the last things an entrepreneur considers when starting up a new business. After all, a company with a handful of employees working for a common economic goal...a paycheck, does not have the same veneer as the workplace climate at a multinational conglomerate with thousands of employees.

But a recent survey of human relations managers indicated that being the target of an employee's lawsuit should be a top consideration of any start-up firm...maybe even the first consideration. The survey, by the Society for Human Resource Management, found that 53 percent of company managers had been named as defendants in at least one employment-related lawsuit and that former employees filed nine out 10 of those suits. Additionally, current employees had sued 37 percent of the companies responding to the survey...and unsuccessful candidates for employment had sued eight percent of them.

A paper trail of negative performance reviews really doesn't matter either. One manager received a summary judgment in a federal court, but then was forced to fight the former employee through a federal appeals court even though the company was able to produce years of documentation showing the worker was a slacker.

Boomers' parents were more tolerant. They expected to be on the job for their whole life. However, with the new work force, employees expect to work for up to eight different employers during their working career; so it's not shocking that they will be quicker to pull the trigger (of a lawsuit). They don't have any expectation of working there their whole life.

The litigation trend may also be occurring, in part, because employees no longer feel loyalty to employers. Baby Boomers differ from their parents because abiding loyalty has gone the way of the phonograph.

Some of my favorites:

> Stella Liebeck, the 81 year-old New Mexico resident who successfully sued McDonald's for $2.7 million for spilling hot coffee in her lap...while driving. She was attempting to remove the spill proof lid from the container (in an effort to add cream and sugar) even as she was negotiating traffic...enough said.

> A federal judge recently threw out a lawsuit alleging that food from McDonald's restaurants was responsible for making people obese. The judge went on to say, "Those who overindulge in

oversized value meals should know there's a health risk associated with their eating habits. It is not a function of society to protect them from their own excesses." And I would say, "There's already a naturally occurring mechanism in place to assist those individual in accepting their responsibilities in such matters...instead of relying on society to shield and guide them. And yes, it's called 'common sense' and I'm sure you remember it from earlier in this book."

The Illinois Court of Appeals has determined that the parents of a child burned by hot tea could sue the Chinese restaurant...even though their child caused the burn by wildly spinning a Lazy Susan around and around. Irresponsible parents again...

Elizabeth Shelton, 21, recently filed a lawsuit in Houston against the truck driver that she accidentally rear-ended in a 2007 crash, while she was intoxicated, and in which her boyfriend was killed. Though she was convicted of manslaughter, she is now suing for $20,000 damage to her Lexus SUV and for "pain and suffering," basing her claim on the fact that the blameless driver she hit was uninsured. In all, her lawsuit names 16 defendants, including insurance companies and banks. Shelton is the daughter of a state court judge. And wouldn't you just know it...again, like parent...like daughter.

But my favorite: In October, 2003, an unidentified man reportedly filed a lawsuit in Selkirk, Manitoba, against the woman who allegedly caused him great mental distress by suing him for back child support. The man "claimed" he had been sound asleep during the 2006 encounter, but awoke to discover the woman having sex with him. He ordered her to "cease and desist," he said, and she complied...but nonetheless, a pregnancy resulted.

And when publicly questioned about the motivation for initiating his or her lawsuit, the plaintiff will then... invariably, insult our intelligence by responding by with, "I'm doing this so that no one else will have to go through what I've been through."

I can't remember being aware of any lawsuits while growing up in my little rural Arkansas community, possibly due to the absence of the above mentioned drivers...but there must have been one or two. My guess is that there probably wasn't a surplus of attorneys and those country folks (with their common senses) were...for the most part, responsible and accountable...and that, along with an honest, eyeball-to-eyeball handshake was enough to settle most disagreements.

The handshake and its firmness, which in another time vouched for your character and sealed bonds between men, have been reduced to a fist bump. In today's "me world" the only thing it represents is "being in" and/or "being current"...character is only a mind game played by the mindless on today's stage.

CHAPTER 8

Anomie is defined as a state of relative "normlessness" or a state in which norms have been eroded. A norm is an expectation of how people will behave, and it takes the form of a rule that is socially rather than formally enforced. Thus, in structural functionalist theory, the effect of normlessness whether at a personal or societal level, is to introduce alienation, isolation and de-socialization, as norms become less binding for individuals. Individuals thus lose the sense of what is right and wrong.

The concept of anomie was later expanded to describe an emerging state of social deregulation where the norms or rules that regulated people's expectations as to how they ought to behave, with each other, were eroding and people no longer knew what to expect from one another. In early, non-specialized societies, people pooled their labor for the production of the necessities for the survival of the whole. They tended to behave and think alike as they worked to achieve group-oriented goals. When societies became more complex, work became more specialized, and social bonds grew more impersonal as the culture shifted from altruism to economic where labor was exchanged for money. Individuals found it difficult to establish their status and role in society without clear norms to guide them. If conditions changed quickly, say during great prosperity or a great depression, the social system came under pressure and the erosion of existing norms without clear alternatives led to dissatisfaction, conflict, and deviance. Thus, the original meaning of anomie did not refer to a state of mind, but to a property of the social structure in which individual desires are no longer regulated by common norms and where, as a consequence, individuals are left without moral guidance in the pursuit of their goals.

The connotation was later, once again, expanded to refer to a morally deregulated personal condition leading to suicide...suggesting that this normlessness also produces psychological effects. There is both personal anxiety and a disruption in the rhythm of social life as economic status and family anomie grows in the face of normlessness and powerlessness. It was first postulated, and then more modern research confirmed, that social anomie could be translated into behavioral (attempted suicide), and attitudinal (normlessness and powerlessness) determinants when viewed with regard to its impact upon the family. Particularly among the young, there are significant differences in the degree of normlessness and powerlessness for suicidal and non-suicidal adolescents and their families.

There is no doubt that our world is in a state of escalating anomie...just look around. But wait, I must add a disclaimer, if you're under 45 or 50 you're probably going to say, "What are you talking about, everything seems pretty normal to me." Well, that takes us back to one of my favorite arguing points...the reality of perspective.

Perspective is, in fact, reality to the individual...based on his or her point of reference and the various life-influencing experiences that came together to craft their perspectives. So with that said, I would suggest that our younger citizens today do not possess the knowledge, wisdom, insight or life experiences to develop a comprehensive perspective. But with our ever-growing youth population, and their tendency to conform to current, evolving social norms (whatever they may be), their perspectives will become the new reality and normlessness will become acceptable as society's new norm. Again, progress...

It seems to me (there's that perspective thing again) that our society is becoming more and more impersonal. Too many folks appear to be preoccupied as they're rushing to and fro with their glazed over eyes focused straight ahead and/or cast downward. Eye contact is very often avoided and when confronted with a smile or a pleasant "Hi" or "How are you doing," they more often than not, react tentatively...even uncomfortably.

We all understand and accept that life recycles various things, tangibles such as clothing fashions, hairstyles, vehicles and even the intangibles like names, words and movie themes. So what I'm suggesting is that perhaps we're currently in an early phase of returning (recycling) to tribalism. We all have ancestors who lived their lives as part of a tribe, and for some of us, that may even be the case today, but for most in the western world, our tribal past was many generations ago.

There are good and bad aspects to traditional tribal culture. On the one hand, a member of a tribe knew where he or she belonged. The traditional tribe is a relatively small and intimate community when compared with modern western culture. This intimacy provides a level of psychological security. The traditional tribe is culturally homogeneous. This is to say that everyone in the tribe believes in the same things. The social rules are consistent from member to member and modes of behavior, dress, play, and work are the same. This adds to the feeling of security and safety. It leads to a strong sense of self as identified with a particular tribe.

On the other hand, traditional tribal membership is restricted by blood, ethnicity, and geography. A down side to this is that sometimes a person is born into a tribe with interests and maybe a destiny that lies outside of the tribal culture. For this person the intimacy and homogeneity of the culture can feel like a prison. Their individuality is challenged and they may be pressured to conform or move on.

In American culture today, we have a somewhat different situation. Although there is a general culture to which we can feel we belong, it has become impersonal and is becoming increasingly fragmented. This is mostly because of the sheer size of country and population. It is possible to be relatively intimate with people in numbers under 1 or 2 thousand, but try being intimate with 300 million.

In looking back 50 to 65 years ago, my little hometown tribe (metaphorically speaking) was pretty representative of our country. We had fewer tribes then because we were less ethnically diverse; we didn't seem to take politics as seriously as folks do today and of course most of us were Christians. But one could beg to differ and say that we did in fact have more than one tribe back then... the American Indians, the Caucasians and the African Americans.

And of course that was before the generation gap, a popular term used to describe differences between people of a younger generation and their elders, especially between a child and his or her parent's generation. The term first became popularized in Western countries during the 1960s and described the cultural differences between the young and their parents.

We're all a part of the USA Tribe, but the layers of sub-tribes run deep. I see the first split as running along chronological age lines and within each of those age groups, perhaps the multitude of various ethnic groups and their cultures therein. But the biggest and most divisive divides are the political and religious ideology differences within those ethnic groups and their cultures.

But there's an even bigger lack of understanding between the young and the old (young and old used subjectively). The young often view the old as out of touch with reality (remember perspective equates to reality) and the old view the young as out of control and without a clue about reality. This of course is not a new conflict between the generations; it has been an on going battle-of-the-wills ever since that second generation caveman suggested, to his father, that they could take that woolly mammoth down with some sharpened sticks instead of gang tackling it.

This brings me back to my accusation about a segment of our population becoming somewhat impersonal. I see it as a manifestation of the younger tribes where ethnicity, culture, political views and religious affiliation still influence their overall make-up, but where the majority are consumed by their addiction to modern day electronic gadgets. Their lives revolve around their cell phones and everything stops if a text or call is in coming. It matters not that they're crossing a busy street, driving a car, working on their job, in a movie theater or having dinner with friends...they're going to respond to that phone...even checking it every few minutes to make sure they haven't missed a "phantom" call or text.

So is it any wonder that they're becoming more impersonal to anyone outside their tribe where conversing is usually facilitated with a few quick, expressionless keystrokes? And making eye contact isn't required during texting... it works for them because their tribes don't understand the importance of eye contact in the real world. Texting has officially been acknowledged as an addiction that is affecting an entire generation. One has to wonder if in another generation...will these tribes be lacking in their ability to communicate face-to-face...competently?

But at the other end of my assertion regarding our younger generation's impersonal demeanor, I would be remiss if I didn't at least postulate the flipside of my allegation. It appears (again, from my perspective) that our older, departing generation has distanced itself from today's modern world with its high-tech, fast-moving, non-compliant culture. I think they (we) struggle with what they perceive as normlessness in a world they no longer recognize, understand or can even relate to. I also believe their method of coping is to withdraw from the frontlines and live within the safety of their self-defining comfort zones. So when you see those folks looking straight ahead...sometimes even with vacant eyes, please give them the benefit of your doubt...they're just trying to co-exist. If anything...perhaps you could just say, "Hello, how are you doing." They will appreciate your gesture and you will feel better for having acknowledged their existence.

The evolution of mankind will continue unabated, because it is an innate survival mechanism. Progress will continue to amaze...and baffle the passing generations. A hundred years from now I can just hear the old folks asking, "What's with these spaced-out teenagers today? They don't even text us anymore since they've gotten into that new trendy obsession where they communicate telepathically. And you never know where they're at or even where they're going now a days...they all seem to have their own personal molecular teleportation devices."

And so it goes...

CHAPTER 9

It seems that just about everyone can tell stories about horrible behavior they've seen in public. Many believe civility is dying, and there's plenty of ammunition out there to support that belief. We text behind the wheel (while driving like dingbats), talk on our cell phones in the checkout line, over dinner with friends, during movies, whenever and wherever...

It's not my intent to relentlessly rag on today's younger generation; I'm merely continuing my comparison between yesteryear and today's accelerated world, and punctuating the differences by dissecting society's general attitude and disposition. Metropolitan inhabitances seem to be the ones most caught-up in today's wired, uptight, sometimes almost frantic lifestyle. But we're all incrementally morphing even as we're being dragged along with or without our consent, and in most cases... without our knowledge. Like an unstoppable glacier with its stealth-like shifting, life as we have known it for generations is slipping away from us. And most don't even realize that it (progress) is on the move and rapidly becoming the new norm...replacing the no-less undesirable, normlessness.

One of the most glaring and defining characteristics of this incoming, replacement norm is its propensity toward non-compliance. By non-compliant I'm not only referring to the various common sense regulations already in place, but the ever growing list of laws that we (as a civilized society) must continue to enact as today's "me" culture pushes the limits of civility.

"Traditionally," we have long embraced...and adhered to, certain common courtesies affecting our day-to-day business and personal interactions with others; but those courtesies and good manners are being battered as our new, progressive way of life gains momentum in its effort to replace our old-school past.

It matters not whether they are family, friends, co-workers, or "others," the old-school saying is that we should treat others, as we would have them treat us.

In its continuing effort to rein in this non-compliant element in our communities, our government legislates more and more laws intended to force compliance. Many of our new laws and regulations are just supplanting everyday, common sense and our traditional, tried and true...self-facilitating, social order. But since we're not enforcing the laws we already have on the books (prioritized based on man-power), the new laws are just lip service and the non-compliant folk promptly realize that the odds are in their favor and they quickly return to their self-indulgent ways.

We all know those traffic laws that are near the bottom of officers' priorities (and of course one of the biggies is cell phone usage while driving), because we see the scofflaws getting away with them everyday...even as we're complying. I see no need to enumerate the infractions that we've all seen, and even have stories about the accidents and/or near accidents caused by non-compliant individuals.

Cell phones are symbolic of today's incivility. Even after being reminded...you can almost count on it, without fail, at least one phone will ring during the movie, at church, in the library, at dinner with friends and even at weddings and funerals.

Cell phones are everywhere. Young and old alike have them, and it's hard to conceive that these folks ever survived without one. Yet this ubiquitous gadget is now a lightning rod for uncivil behavior.

A friend of mine, knowing I was writing on this subject, shared a story regarding his experience at an upscale New Jersey restaurant. It seems that a woman's cell phone went off at a nearby table...and predictably, the woman answered the phone.

But here's the rub. At that particular restaurant, the waiters were opera singers who performed between courses. A baritone was in mid-song when the phone rang...and amazingly, the woman started talking louder and louder to be heard over the music. Well, within seconds, the restaurant's owner physically picked her up and removed her from the establishment. And to the credit of the owner and his other customers, he received a standing ovation.

As tough as this medicine maybe to swallow, sometimes the best thing to do while in public is to not answer your phone...or better yet, have it turned off. It's also impolite to answer the phone during a casual dinner at a friend's house, but people routinely...and without a second thought, not only answer their phones but engage in lengthy conversations. In someone else's home, you should have your cell phone turned off (unless you're expecting an important call); it would be as though you've invited someone else to come along with you for dinner at your friend's house.

Due to the explosion of cell phone use, doctors, dentists and other professionals have been forced to post signs in their offices asking people to refrain from using their cell phones. It is disruptive to staff and affects the flow of work.

There is an appropriate time and place to answer a cell phone call, but there may be a generational difference of opinion in what is considered an appropriate time and/or place.

Talking quietly while waiting in a long line is fine, but using the cell phone in front of a store clerk is rude. It's important to make sure you are being respectful to others when you're on the phone. Taking long phone calls while out with friends or frequently texting at the table certainly can be perceived as rude. It should always be about being respectful to those around you.

It is incredibly ironic, that the very technology that enables people to be constantly connected with others can also result in their being disconnected from those around them. The convenience of communication, the ability to whip out your cell phone...it just seems to outweigh the notion that might suggest...wait, perhaps I should do this later where I won't bother or disturb others.

But there's another group of non-compliant slackers amongst us as we make our way through traffic each and everyday. These people, not unlike the ones in the preceding paragraphs, also view their time and needs as more important than any inconvenience their actions may cause others. Their maneuvers may or may not be illegal in the truest sense, but it's almost always a personal, selfish, inconsiderate act driven by their lack of common courtesies. Again, we have all experienced these "citizens"...for lack of a more fitting term, but I will, in this case, share a few examples:

> I've seen individuals (more than once) hold up three lanes of traffic as they tried to make their way from the far right into the left-turn lane at the last minute. Because they had been on their cell phone (non-compliantly) the preceding couple of miles they hadn't made the conscious decision to move over in preparation for their left-hand turn into the coffee shop on the opposite side of the boulevard. You or I, being courteous and not wanting to inconvenience others...due to our lack of forethought, would have continued down the street and around the block as we circled back to Starbucks. But that's usually not the option that the non-compliant choose to run with.

> I remember when a car's flashing turn signal was a request...seeking permission to change lanes and merge into yours (yes, I'm that old). But today that flashing taillight is a statement saying, "Just letting you know that I'm already halfway into your lane and you need to back off because you're now tailgating me." Of course if they're just turning left or right, chances are that you won't see a signal at all.

We also have the "Speed Racers" on our streets and highways, cutting in and out of traffic (without signaling), tailgating and all the while giving any and everyone who impedes their progress, the evil eye. I could see Speed Racer in my rearview mirror weaving from lane to lane as he worked his way through the moderate mid-day traffic. He made his way up to my rear bumper before darting around me on the right (as he gave me a look of disdain) before squeezing in between the two cars ahead of me. Shortly thereafter I saw him work his way back into the lane just to the left of me... the same lane he was in when I first noticed him behind me. I lost interest in his whereabouts after he moved away from me, but a few blocks later as I was coming to a stop at a four-way signal... well lo and behold, wouldn't you just know it, I had stopped right along side Speed Racer. And of course I received another look from him, but this time it was more of an inquisitive look...as in, "How'd you do that?"

Another area of declining civility and social order is in the gray, unregulated regions of each individual's consciousness regarding social responsibilities and the acknowledgment that their actions...or lack of, can affect others (we do not live in a vacuum), which appears to be a very one-sided concept today. And again, I will list a few examples:

In recent years, restaurants in my neighborhood (Orange County) have ceased accepting unsecured reservations; a credit card is now required for what used to be a common courtesy. Due to the increasing number of socially irresponsible individuals who not only become "no-shows," they don't even bother to call and cancel so that others can be accommodated. So now, because of "them," we must all provide a credit card number, over the phone, to make dinner reservations. In today's world of scamming, card-swiping and identity theft, the last thing I want to do with my card is to give that number to someone on the phone when I can't be sure of their intentions.

Returning a phone call (personal or business) used to be a given, but today it seems that the odds of them actually getting back to us are about 50/50. One would think that with today's cell phone usage that a return call would be almost automatic... go figure. Of course calls to "customer service" (an oxymoron today) numbers account for a large portion of the non-returned calls. You can't speak to a real person anymore and the menus on their voicemails run you around and around until you give up and/or leave a message, which all too often represents nothing more than an exercise in futility, as there will probably be no follow-up call to you...the customer.

Supermarkets (again, in my neighborhood) are being forced, though legislation of course, to take responsibility for the carts that the irresponsible general public pushes home. They then unload their groceries and leave the pushcarts sitting on their sidewalks and/or streets, thereby creating a nuisance and eyesores. The stores are now required to place locking devises on the wheels that will somehow keep the carts from being taken home, they are also expected to pay for the cost of retrieving any wayward carts that for whatever reason escape the confines of the shopping mall. So rather than place the blame where it belongs, we'll hang it on the storeowners because we can't enforce it against the real offenders. So guess who will be footing the bill for the negligent actions of yet another group of the socially irresponsible... of course, the rest of us. That additional cost will most certainly be passed on to the consumer.

I know that I should leave this next issue alone, but it's the reality of our world...not just our country. I absolutely accept and believe that discrimination (age and/or gender) and racism is a real and problematic divide. But in our ever increasingly, politically correct world, it has become a crutch, a social and political tool that drives the entitlement mentality. It influences frivolous lawsuits, provides excuses for the irresponsible, and justification for those deemed accountable. As a society, we encourage a "victim-hood mentality" and an overweening government that never met an issue it didn't want to dive into with both feet; so we shouldn't be surprised that so many Americans expect to be rewarded for failures.

A good rule of thumb when navigating today's world of movers and shakers, is to understand that their take on life is that being next is no longer acceptable, they're entitled to be first.

And don't even get me started on the habitually offended...

CHAPTER 10

The neurotic assumes too much responsibility...while the person with a character disorder assumes too little. When neurotics are in conflict with the world, they automatically presume that they are at fault. When those with character disorders are in conflict with the world, they automatically presume the world is at fault.

I'll probably be severely challenged on this one, but it's my old-school opinion and I must voice my thoughts on one last area of accountability...financial responsibility.

Growing up in Arkansas, I was told...more than once, that if we couldn't pay cash for an item, we could probably live without it. But I'm not suggesting that that mentality could fly in today's more affluent world. I'm just setting the table for what may be another less-than-palatable serving of perspective (mine)...there's that word again.

Doctor Spock advocated ideas about parenting that were, at the time, considered out of the mainstream. Over time, his books helped to bring about a major change, if not a reversal, in the opinions of those who considered themselves to be the experts. Previously, experts had told parents that babies needed to learn to sleep on a regular schedule and that picking them up and holding them whenever they cried would only teach them to cry more and not to sleep through the night (a notion that borrowed from behaviorism). They were told to feed their children on a regular schedule, and that they should not pick them up, kiss them, or hug them, because that would not prepare them to be strong and independent individuals in a harsh world. Spock encouraged parents to see their children as individuals, and not to apply a one-size-fits all philosophy to them.

At the time of its publication, Baby and Child Care appeared to emphasize permissiveness in child rearing, in striking contrast to earlier child rearing guides that stressed harsher discipline. His advice fit the mood of the time, which was geared toward a more pleasurable domestic life. In the years since his book became a bestseller, he has been lionized for having made child rearing more professional and for providing new parents with self-confidence. But on the other hand, critics have blamed him for contributing to an unhealthy child-centeredness that they felt produced guilt-ridden mothers and spoiled children. Since the 1960s, feminists have assailed him for making women believe that they were fully responsible for their children's development and that full-time mothering was essential; conservatives have held him responsible for what they have believed to be the misbehavior of the youth of the sixties who were reared according to his "permissive" formulas.

Many seeing Spock as the leader in the movement toward more permissive parenting, in general, have long blamed him for what they perceive as being the negative fallout.

Norman Vincent Peale claimed in the late 1960s that the U.S. was paying a price for the two generations that followed the Dr. Spock baby plan of "instant gratification of wants." Vice President Spiro Agnew once denounced him as the "father of permissiveness," claiming that Spock's child rearing principles encouraged lawlessness among young people in the 1960s.

We've spent decades trying to pump up the self-esteem of children in our public schools, regardless of whether they did anything to merit it...or not.

In the summer of 2005, a retired British schoolteacher proposed a rather controversial motion to her union, the Professional Association of Teachers (PAT). She suggested that the word failure should be banned from classrooms and replaced with the more palatable phrase "deferred success" so as not to discourage students from continuing efforts to achieve. Although the motion ultimately experienced its own "deferred success," it was not without supporters among the 35,000-member teacher's association. Another member of the organization expressed his enthusiastic agreement...saying, "It's time we made the word fail redundant and replaced it with please do a bit more." The words fail or failure, it seems, are not good for building self-esteem in school children.

The same year, several American newspapers reported that the newest threat to children's self-esteem was the use of red ink in public schools. According to one Utah paper, parents objected to the use of red ink on the grounds that it was too "stressful." The school responded by banning the offending color. Now, The Utah Morning News says, "Blue and other colors are in."

A year earlier, the word from the Boston Globe was that purple reigned supreme. "A mix of red and blue, the color purple embodies red's sense of authority but also blue's association with serenity, making it a less negative and more constructive color for correcting student papers. The color psychologists said, "Purple calls attention to itself without being too aggressive. And because the color is linked to creativity and royalty, it is also more encouraging to students."

Stories like these are not new, nor are they simply British and American phenomena. Parents and teachers throughout the West have been interested in building self-esteem in children for nearly half a century.

Of course, it isn't as though the concept of self-esteem wasn't around before the 1960s. In fact, a Harvard psychologist named William James developed a formula for it as early as 1890. Earlier definitions of self-esteem, however, bear little resemblance to recently popularized versions. James suggested that how we feel about ourselves in this world depends entirely on what we believe ourselves to be capable of, and what we do with that capability. It is determined by the ratio of our actualities to our supposed potentialities, and he went so far as to portray this ratio as a literal fraction.

It would be nearly three-quarters of a century before another psychologist revisited the concept with any significant interest. But even Stanley Coopersmith, who proposed in 1967 that building self-esteem was a child-rearing necessity, underscored that the parents of children with high self-esteem were the kind who set clear limits and defined high standards of behavior, modeling these by their own examples.

Somewhere in intervening years, however, the "doing well" aspect of building self-esteem seemed gradually to lose ground to the "feeling good" part of the message.

Armies of teachers and parents are straining to bolster children's self-esteem. And while that sounds innocuous enough, the way they do it often erodes children's sense of worth. By emphasizing how a child feels, at the expense of what the child does...mastery, persistence, overcoming frustration and boredom, and meeting challenge...parents and teachers are making this generation of children more vulnerable to depression.

How could it be that well-meaning attempts to shield children from feeling bad could actually result in more depression rather than less?

The most obvious pitfall lies in dishonesty. It should go without saying that encouragement is a good thing. Praise, when merited, can be a wonderful tool for reinforcing positive action. But children see through empty praise, however well meaning it is, and on the basis of such deceit can begin to mistrust even deserved praise.

Another pitfall lies in the belief that children must be protected from failure and the resulting bad feelings... both of which are necessary steps in the learning process. In order for your child to experience mastery, it is necessary for him to fail, to feel bad, and to try again repeatedly until success occurs. None of these steps can be circumvented. Failure and feeling bad are necessary building blocks for ultimate success and feeling good.

In 1990, California published a report claiming that poor self-esteem is the cause of such ills as academic failure, drug use, teenage pregnancy and dependence on welfare. However, after having produced the assessment, the report could only give vague recommendations for solutions. Why...?

Because there is no effective technology for teaching feeling good that does not first teach doing well. Feelings of self-esteem in particular and happiness in general, develop as side effects...of mastering challenges, working successfully, overcoming frustration and boredom and winning. The feelings of self-esteem are a byproduct of doing well.

The conclusion is that similar approaches to that of the 1990 California report will always have the cart before the horse. If we, as parents and teachers promote the doing-well side of self-esteem, the feeling-good side that cannot be taught directly, will follow. What California (and every state) needs is not children who are encouraged to feel good, but children who are taught the skills of doing well...how to study, how to avoid pregnancy, drugs, and gangs, and how to get off welfare.

These skills are foundational to doing well, and students will be most effectively educated if coached by their earliest role models...their own parents, because they have a vested interest in their children's psychological well-being.

It seems that over the past five or six decades that a slowly evolving trend (progress) has changed yet another facet of society. The increasing growth of permissiveness as parents, an emerging culture of instant gratification, and a tradition of artificially instilling misguided self-esteem in our young has changed the complexion of our way of life.

Today's parents are, too often, attempting to treat their children as friends instead of parenting them. And in that endeavor, boundaries become skewed and roles can become conflicted...causing rebelliousness and long-term problems for all concerned.

For the most part, we all have more (financially & materialistically) than our parents ever amassed. Because we have more, we have more to give our broods in wanting them to have yet an even better life than we built. But by giving each generation more and more, how much have we contributed to their instant gratification behavior...and their materialistic traits?

And getting back to those self-worth issues...are today's instant gratification, over-indulgent, and materialistic individuals still working on their adolescent self-esteem issues?

One more analogy, could today's economic meltdown be another symptom of the masses stroking their fragile self-esteem? The foreclosures on houses that they couldn't afford in the first place, driving their gas guzzling SUVs, credit cards maxed out...and still buying name brands.

Financial responsibility, once a cornerstone of yesteryear, has become yet another casualty of today's progress.

It's great to have a healthy self-image, but there's not much to be said for thinking you're smarter than the collective wisdom and traditions passed down through human history just because you happen to read the Daily Kos.

CHAPTER 11

Fortunately my livelihood doesn't depend on the success of my writing; I just enjoy seeing my name on the cover of books. Of course it also affords me the opportunity to utilize many of those southern sayings that I heard as a kid growing up in Arkansas. So with that said, I would suggest that "we" pay attention when an old dog is barking...

Book readership has been in steady decline for years now and there is a general consensus, well...it's my opinion anyway, that that decline has been driven by the ever-decreasing attention span of today's Internet addicted culture. I'm just laying this out for consumption as I continue to evaluate, and compare, our ever-changing world and lifestyle...good, bad or whatever.

Attention span is the amount of time a person can concentrate on a task without becoming distracted. Most educators and psychologists agree that the ability to focus one's attention on a task is crucial for the achievement of one's goals. It has even been suggested that "perhaps" because of the Internet, the stunning variety of news sources, and the complexity of our modern, high-tech world, that we've become much less able, as a populace, to follow logical arguments and deal with complex messages and issues.

Attention span varies with age...with older children capable of longer periods of attention than younger children. The type of activity is also an important consideration, as people are generally capable of a longer attention span when they are doing something that they find enjoyable or intrinsically motivating. Estimates for the length of human attention span are highly variable and range from 3 to 5 minutes per year of age in young children, to a maximum of around 20 minutes in adults. Nevertheless, the average movie lasts approximately two hours, and most adults can follow the plot with only minimal lapses of attention.

The attention span of humans is apparently much shorter than it used to be. I would offer as an example, the Lincoln-Douglas debates of 1858. If you remember, they lasted for hours in front of sustained audiences, whereas modern debates do not begin to approach that length. I know that because I've judged Lincoln-Douglas debates many times at our local Christian Colleges.

The instant gratification made possible by modern technology appears to have had a detrimental effect on attention span. One study of 2,600 children found that early exposure to television (around age two) is associated with later attention problems at age seven or eight. Internet browsing may have a similar effect because it enables rapid viewing. Most Internet users spend less than one minute on the average website. It may be wise for parents to limit television and Internet use in children and encourage them to read books instead. A gradual progression to longer books could be an effective way to develop a healthy attention span.

Social network sites risk "infantilizing" the mid-21st century mind, leaving it characterized by short attention spans, sensationalism, the inability to empathize and a shaky sense of identity, according to a leading neuroscientist.

This startling warning has led members of government to admit their work on Internet regulation has not been extended to broader issues, such as the psychological impact on children. Government has yet to look at the broad cultural and psychological effect of on-screen friendships via Facebook, My Yearbook, Tag, Twitter, etc. Children's experiences on social networking sites are devoid of cohesive narrative and/or long-term significance.

Studies are suggesting that social networking sites are putting attention spans in jeopardy as the young brain is exposed, from the beginning, to a world of fast action and reaction, of instant new screen images flashing up with the press of a key, and that such rapid interchange might (over time) acclimatize the brain to an elevated operational level. And perhaps later, in the real world, when appropriate responses are not immediately forthcoming, we will see such behaviors and call them attention-deficit disorder.

It might be helpful to investigate whether the near total submersion of our culture in screen technologies over the last decade might be, in some way, linked to the threefold increase in prescriptions for methylphenidate, the drug prescribed for attention-deficit hyperactivity disorder.

We should also be concerned about the noticeable preference for the here-and-now, where the immediacy of an experience trumps any regard for the consequences. After all, whenever you play a computer game, you can always just play it again; everything you do is reversible. The emphasis is on the thrill of the moment, the buzz of rescuing the princess in the game. No care is given for the princess herself, for the content or for any long-term significance, because there is none. This type of activity, a disregard for consequence, can be compared with the thrill of compulsive gambling or compulsive eating. The sheer compulsion of reliable and almost immediate reward is being linked to similar chemical systems in the brain that may also play a part in drug addiction. So we should not underestimate the pleasure of interacting with a screen when we puzzle over why it seems so appealing to young people.

Research has warned that there is the risk of empathy loss as children read novels less. Unlike the game to rescue the princess, where the goal is to feel rewarded; the aim of reading a book is, after all, to find out more about the princess herself.

I find it strange that we are enthusiastically embracing the possible erosion of our identities through social networking sites, since those that use such sites can lose a sense of where they themselves finish and the outside world begins. That sense of identity can be eroded by fast-paced, instant screen reactions. Perhaps the next generation will define themselves by the responses of others.

Social networking sites can provide a constant reassurance...that you are listened to, recognized, and important. This is coupled with a distancing from the stress of face-to-face, real-life conversation, which are far more perilous...occur in real time, with no opportunity to think up clever or witty responses and require a sensitivity to voice tone, body language and perhaps even to pheromones...those sneaky molecules that we release and which others smell subconsciously.

I have often wondered if real conversation in real time may eventually give way to these sanitized and easier screen dialogues, in much the same way as killing, skinning and butchering an animal to eat has been replaced by the convenience of packages of meat on the supermarket shelf. It is conceivable that future generations will recoil with similar horror at the messiness, unpredictability and immediate personal involvement of a three-dimensional, real-time interaction.

Some have argued that the appeal of Facebook lies in the fact that a child confined to the home every evening may find, on the keyboard, the kind of freedom of interaction and communication that earlier generations took for granted in their three-dimensional world on the outside. But even given a choice, screen life can still be more appealing to this current creation.

I read where one user was boasting about having over 900 friends; and another saying that the fact you can't see or hear other people makes it easier to reveal yourself in a way that you might not otherwise be comfortable with. You become less conscious of the individuals involved (including yourself), less inhibited, less embarrassed and less concerned about how you will be viewed or evaluated.

It is hard to see how living this way, on a daily basis, will not result in brains and/or minds differing immensely from those of previous generations. We know that the human brain is exquisitely sensitive to the outside world.

Family togetherness time is absorbing the immediate brunt of the Internet as family use has soared. Whether it's around the dinner table or just in front of the TV, U.S. families say they are spending less time together. The decline in family time coincides with a rise in Internet use and the popularity of social networks, though a new study stopped just short of assigning blame.

A recent study out of the University of Southern California reported that 28 percent of Americans it interviewed last year (2008) said they had been spending less time with members of their households. That's nearly triple the 11 percent who said that in 2006.

These people did not report spending less time with their friends, however.

A senior fellow at the center, said people reported spending less time with family members just as social networks like Facebook, Twitter and MySpace began booming, along with the importance people were placing on them. Five-year-old Facebook's active user base, for example, has surged to more than 200 million active users, up from 100 million last August.

Meanwhile, more people say they are worried about how much time kids and teenagers are spending online. In 2000, when the center began its annual surveys on Americans and the Internet, only 11 percent of respondents said that family members under 18 were spending too much time online. By 2008, that grew to 28 percent.

Most people think of the Internet and (our) digital future as boundless, and I do too, but it can't be a good thing that families are spending less face-to-face time together. Ultimately it will lead to less cohesive and less communicative families.

The advent of new technologies has, in many ways, always changed the way family members interact. Cell phones make it easier for parents to keep track of where their children are, while giving them the kind of privacy they wouldn't have had in the days of landlines.

Television has cut into dinnertime, and as TV sets became cheaper, they also multiplied, so that kids and parents no longer have to congregate in the living room to watch it.

Because the Internet is so engrossing, and demands so much more attention than other technologies, it can disrupt personal boundaries in ways other technologies wouldn't have. It's not like television, where you can sit around with your family and just watch it...the Internet is mostly one-on-one.

Likely because they can afford more Web-connected gadgets, higher-income families reported greater loss of family time than those who make less money. And more women than men said they felt ignored by a family member using the Internet.

Those who make the worst use of their time are the first to complain of its shortness. And now you know who "they" are...

CHAPTER 12

Daniel Defoe, early eighteenth century novelist (Robinson Crusoe), pamphleteer, and part-time spy, is usually credited with the first use of some form of the phrase about the certainty of both death and taxes. Benjamin Franklin borrowed from Defoe and refined it: "In this world nothing can be said to be certain, except death and taxes."

We talk a lot these days about taxes...maybe too much. But we certainly don't talk enough about death, except when someone famous and/or beloved passes on. How many times have you heard the idea that bad things come in "threes?" Well, Ed McMahon passed the other day, as did Farrah Fawcett, and then came the death of pop icon Michael Jackson. The first two events had seemed to be sadly imminent for sometime, one because of chronic health issues driven by age while the other succumbed after a valiantly fought, but losing battle with cancer. Mr. McMahon was 86, the former Charlie's Angel was 62 and Michael was 50.

And what about Gale Storm's recent passing...? I happened to stumble across a two-paragraph article regarding her death buried in the back of my local newspaper. During the 50s she starred in "My Little Margie" and "The Gale Storm Show," and appeared in numerous B movies opposite such stars as Roy Rogers, Eddie Albert and Jackie Cooper. But those wholesome types are passé today, as in...insignificant and irrelevant. Yesteryear...

But on the front page of my local newspaper, I read that a White House adviser had reported (on NBC's "Meet the Press") that President Barack Obama had written to the Jackson family to express his condolences. I then had to ask myself, why the Jackson family and not the McMahon or Fawcett family. But of course the answer is a no-brainer...constituency, it's all about his constituency. Today's generation...

And of course the Jackson family was outraged that Michael's sordid past was "touched on" by some of the media outlets. The recapping of his life, for the purpose of news releases, was no different than any other celebrity's passing...if anything, the media did tread very lightly on his strange and troubled life. The accusations and pay-offs have long been common knowledge.

I can't help but think about Stephen Johns, the kind and generous security guard who opened a door at the Holocaust Museum recently, only to be gunned down by a hateful excuse of a man. And just a few weeks ago, a young Army enlistee was gunned down in front of a recruiting office where he had volunteered to work while waiting for deployment to Iraq...the shooter was a home grown Islamic extremist. Where was the public's outpouring of grief, sorrow and sympathy for these and many other deserving individuals?

Of course, our morning newspapers are filled with death notices, names that mean something to relatively few as compared to what happens when someone famous dies. So, why is it that so many find themselves moved...even a little emotional, when they hear about the passing of someone they only knew from afar? Is it just because of the whole overdone 24/7-news coverage, looping stuff over and over and talking ad infinitum (a Latin phrase meaning "to infinity") about a person?

I actually think something else is at play here. Something deeper. Something instinctive. Something that is directly tied to how we are all wired. Centuries ago, a king whose name is synonymous with wisdom, but who actually did a lot of dumb things...reflected: "Better to spend your time at funerals than at parties. After all, everyone dies...so the living should take this to heart. Sorrow is better than laughter, for sadness has a refining influence on us. A wise person thinks a lot about death, while a fool thinks only about having a good time."

Solomon wasn't talking about some kind of morbid fascination with the details of death. He was referring to the quite healthy idea of stopping and thinking through, the real and profound meaning of death. It is the ultimate area for personal reflection. We can all identify with dying, death, and grief...in some way, whether we'll admit it or not.

As I watched bits and pieces of the around the clock coverage of the passing of Michael Jackson, I found myself somewhat moved, but not because I was a big fan...far from it. I liked some of the old Jackson Five stuff and when he sang to that rodent named Ben, but as he grew up and drifted further out there, I just lost interest. This is not meant to demean or disparage the deceased...we were just different generations.

I also hope that moments like this will help all of us think about what life means and what death really encompasses. We all have birth certificates (those of us who can find them), but I have never seen one with an expiration date. Death comes to all shapes, sizes, colors, and at any time and any place...but make no mistake, it will find you.

I, of course, have (at my age) attended many funerals including, but not limited to, my parents, my siblings, relatives, in-laws, close friends and associates. Their ages and all the other possible parameters ran the full gamut. A grieving mother accepting the flag for her son, a Vietnam vet who took his own life, brought tears...as Taps played in the background.

I have, on occasion, shared words of comfort as best I could, but always with the nagging sense that they fell short, because...well, they did. Being a human being, I have wept, even when my tears were tempered by my Christian faith and hope. Jesus himself wept, though knowing that his deceased friend, Lazarus, would momentarily rejoin the living.

Do I think celebrity-driven grief is overdone? Yes... absolutely, but I know it is easy for some to become myopic these days, obsessed with something out of proportion to how it actually impacts their individual lives. I also find myself somewhat put off by our current generation's shallow determination of human worth...for them, it's all about superficial show...substance just never seems to enter their evaluation process.

You see, when I think of Ed McMahon's passing, I think of my elders, some who have long since left this earth, and others who are moving toward that inevitable moment. When I think of Farrah Fawcett, I can't help but think of my mother, who passed many years ago in her early 60s, after a lengthy and valiant battle with cancer and alcoholism.

What do I think of when I focus on Michael Jackson's passing? I think of a little boy with such talent, and then the man he grew into. He was obviously someone who struggled with an assortment of emotional and psychological abnormalities during his life, and seemed to have so many unhappy moments, in spite of a global fan-base and the fleeting nature of material success.

As a student of history...and as an amateur historian, as well...I know that there is a time and place for the analyzing of one's life, be it good, bad and/or ugly. But it's not during the memorial or wake. There should be a time and space to mourn, especially for those who really knew him. At this point it would be unseemly to sift cynically through the man's life, although I imagine there is a lot there that would not match my values. But history will be written later, revealing some things while clouding others...but there will always be lingering questions. Was Michael Jackson a bad or good person? I have my thoughts (rooted in scripture), while others may think differently. But that he was a broken and hurting person, most would agree. When Jesus announced his ministry in Capernaum, he did not indicate that he was on the scene to root out the bad people, but he did talk a lot about the broken and needy. He also talked about how he wasn't sent to condemn the world, but to redeem it.

For now, the most compelling lesson for us as we note the passing of these famous people is to approach it all like Solomon: "A wise person thinks a lot about death, while a fool thinks only about having a good time."

Well, so much for Solomon's wisdom, personal reflection and a refining influence, Michael's passing has triggered parties and celebrations around the world. Last night's BET Awards Show (Black Entertainment Television) featured highlights from the "iconic" Michael Jackson's illustrious career. And the fools partied on through the night...

Of course there is a "huge" generational divide separating Solomon and Obama's followers.

I've learned it's best to give up all the other worlds, and live only in the one to which I belong...

CHAPTER 13

I realize that I've spent a lot of time bashing today's younger generation(s), but I will acknowledge that it's the bad actors getting all the attention while the good actors go un-noticed...by the general public. They are arbitrarily lumped right in with the irresponsible ne'er-do-wells. This past Friday evening, while attending my granddaughter's high school commencement ceremony, I was reminded that I know some of those good actors. Taylor Robinson is my oldest son's stepdaughter, but he has been her dad since she was an infant.

As we waited for the overflow crowd to make it's way in and get seated, I overheard Taylor's mother conveying an interesting story to her mother (Taylor's grandmother). It seems that about a week before this evening's graduation program, Taylor requested a private meeting with the principal and was given a time slot for their meeting. Taylor was punctual, but the principal arrived late...and I only emphasize this point because I still believe that adults (in leadership positions) should lead by example.

Once the principal appeared, she greeted Taylor and inquired about the nature of their conference. Taylor said, "You do know that my full name is Taylor Robinson, correct?" The principal replied in the affirmative. Taylor then said, "But what you may not know is that Lance Neal has been my dad for most of my life." The principal's face spoke volumes about the emotions Taylor's declaration had resurrected as she softly uttered, "oh." Taylor went on to advise the principal that she would not be shaking her hand, on graduation night, when she stepped forward to accept her diploma. She also explained that she just wanted to get this issue out in the open early to prevent any uncomfortable or awkward moments on stage and/ or in front of, a packed stadium. Again the principal appeared to be caught completely off guard as an almost involuntary retort emerged as she informed Taylor, "You probably don't know everything about that situation (The Path to Addiction)." Taylor, staying on the highroad, simply replied, "I didn't come here today to argue the particulars...or the drivers, for what you did; I'm here because principles matter to me and common courtesy dictates that I not blindside you in that public arena next week." She then thanked the principal for her time and exited the office.

Taylor's silence may have been misinterpreted, but it can never be misquoted...

There were any number of things Taylor could have thrown out, but the family has put the ugliness of that injustice behind them and moved on through that new door that opened as the old door was being unhinged. The local newspaper and football parents supported the coach, but school districts are notorious for not acknowledging their mistakes...they will do whatever it takes to cover their incompetence. They stonewalled until push came to shove...and the last step was binding arbitration. Up until that point all they had to do was deny and stick together, but arbitration would bring in an unbiased outsider to review the evidence and declare a winner... and a loser. The loser would then bear the cost of the hearing, plus the settlement amount (dictated by the presiding arbitrator) and that information would also become public information.

And yes, just days before the impending arbitration process, the district presented a settlement offer (with a confidentiality clause of course) that was accepted, because it represented full vindication.

Now, just a quick re-orientation as I begin mentally and physically reloading for the second leg of my journey, *The Long Road Home...*

The first road trip lasted about six weeks and provided me with the motivation and desire...if not the direction, to examine the possibility of *going home.* Since returning to California, I've spent the past few months writing the preceding chapters based on my thoughts and findings from that initial exploratory trip. I'm now approaching a point in my writing where I feel a need to return to the origin of my hypothetical destination. In the coming weeks I will, once again, launch another extended road trip into my past. While I still have a wealth of unwritten thoughts and subject matter floating around in my head, there are several unanswered questions that I (more than anyone else) would like to lay to rest in this, my last book. Those questions and their answers (assuming I discover the answers) are not going to change anyone's life...they're only lingering details in a mind that's in the counting-down stage of life...mine. The answers, and my theoretical goal can only be uncovered...or buried, in my rural past.

With Norman Rockwell riding shotgun for me, I resumed my search for James Dean and Marlon Brando...knowing full well that my journey is not only an acceptance of where I "sprung" from, but the acknowledgment that perhaps I never left home; I just distanced myself in an effort to seek relevance...but at the end of the day, I've accepted my irrelevance.

Going home is also about one's age and the losses they have accumulated and endured over a lifetime. You rarely hear anyone under 60 talk about *going home*... and I mean that (*going home*) in the truest sense. All too often, as the years fade into times gone by, the pain and loneliness of outliving your family and friends grows and becomes a mentally burdensome existence. So the downside of a long life is that you'll be around to witness the departures of your relatives and acquaintances even as your world grows smaller and smaller. And of course if one lives long enough, that mental burden will most likely be accompanied by its even more demoralizing counterpart...physical encumbrance. As health problems grow, the loss of personal independence and other intangibles (mental and physical fatigue) will, at some point (verbalized or not), fuel a desire to *go home*.

Some would counter that in most cases we still have our children to live for, but I would argue that no parent wants to burden their children...especially at this stage of their life. I would also point out that no parent wants to outlive his or her offspring.

It now seems only appropriate that I, once again, circle by my favorite uncle's place as he is the last of my Mother's family...and as such, the last living link to my Mother.

Those of you who read my first book know why I refer to Milford as my favorite uncle, but you may not know that

I've always believed myself to be his favorite nephew...well, he never exactly told me that, but he has always shared his vehicles with me (it's a guy thing). And his 1931, Model-A, Ford that you read about earlier in this book was no exception. I'm sure you remember back about five months ago when he was showing me around his super-sized garage and we almost fell victim to circumstance. Well, once he managed to get his newest toy pumping out that rich fuel mixture, it came to him that "we" should drive the Model-A down to the Sears store and have them repair that slow leak in the fender-mounted spare tire. I tried to talk him out of the idea...I mean, I really tried to convince him to do it another day (like any day after I left). But he wouldn't hear of it because it wasn't about getting that tire repaired, that I later learned had needed attention for months, it was about taking me for a ride in his prized possession...his time machine.

I reluctantly agreed to accompany him after he weasel-worded me into believing that Sears was just down the road a bit. But my chagrin only grew as we tooled out toward the road..."the interstate!" As we're motoring in the general direction of the fast moving highway I'm still thinking that we'll be utilizing a frontage road to reach our destination...wrong! We did actually turn onto the parallel roadway...but only long enough to reach the interstate's first on-ramp. And...that's where the white-knuckle, Mad Hatter's wild tea cup ride became reality for me. We hit that inside lane at a blistering...or mind numbing, depending on which seat one was occupying, 30 miles an hour. I knew we were a spectacle out there even as my uncle was grinding the gears...working to shift into third, and while he was struggling with the shifting, he was allowing the vehicle to drift to the right... thankfully to the right. I had already witnessed how he fought with the antiquated steering system so I wasn't surprised at the less than smooth course correction...I mean over-correction! But due to a little understanding or defensive driving from the other, "mostly amused," commuters...we were given more latitude than your everyday, normal looking trekkers.

So now we're back in our lane but still slowing down the slow lane traffic when Milford announced he was going to get'er up to 40. I'm thinking okay, that's probably better than having one of these Waco folks (remember Waco?) develop road rage and unload on us. I'm watching the speedometer as we were slowly closing in on the 40 mark, even as the Model-A began to shake just a little, but I didn't say anything because we were so close to 40...the agreed upon speed. But just as we hit 40, my uncle turned to me (while turning the steering wheel as if it was attached to his head) and made yet another declaration of increasing our speed...to 45. So now we're once again drifting to the right even as we're in a snail-like acceleration mode...and that once negligible shaking was now becoming more like an elevated concern. We're now rapidly (relative term of course) approaching a lengthy causeway with guardrails that appeared to be only two or three foot high. While Milford is calmly endeavoring to bring us back on track, I'm thinking we're in trouble...but what scared me the most was that my uncle wasn't sharing my sense of urgency. I was telling myself (you know, not out loud...just thinking it), I've gotta do something or we're going hit that guardrail and roll right over into this lake and die.

I was pretty sure that we were going to be the featured, front-page headliners for the next day's Waco News.

Shades of the *Secondhand Lions:*

> Two old codgers were killed yesterday when they apparently lost control of their vintage automobile while crossing the Lake Waco Causeway. According

to eyewitnesses, who had been following the anomalous couple for several miles, the two men had been traveling erratically and at funeral procession speeds. Another witness added that it appeared that an argument might have contributed to the car crashing into the guardrail and the resulting plunge into the lake below. Divers are onsite today as the search for the bodies continues and officials have indicated they will be looking into the possibility that alcohol or others drugs may have been a dynamic in causing their strange behavior. But the general feeling is that they were just a couple of old geezers trying to reconnect with their youth...and their past before *going home.*

Of course that nightmare didn't actually materialize... but as we exited downtown (yes, we are now down town in heavy traffic) we rolled into yet another predicament. Our highway had intersected with three others and each provided two-lane off-ramps into the downtown traffic below...where we were headed of course. Each off-ramp fed independently into four separate groups of three directional lanes at the bottom and formed a four-way, signal-controlled intersection. As you might imagine, each and every lane was occupied and poised to go at the first glint of a light change...and of course everyone (except my uncle) was in a "me first" hurry. And wouldn't you just know it, we were just lucky enough that our vehicle qualified (based on arrival time) for the "pole" position in our lane...and yes; I knew that we would, sooner or later, be forced to deal with a green light. We're sitting there with this rough idling engine, still in neutral and knowing our go time was very close...and again I'm thinking, why doesn't he already have it in gear and bringing the RPMs up a little in anticipation of getting out with the flow of traffic.

When that long anticipated green light finally gave us (and all those cars behind us) the go-ahead, Milford calmly began the process of engaging the low gear in preparation for moving forward with the pressing traffic. But I had a sick feeling in the pit of my stomach...hence my growing concerns. He was once again grinding the gears even as he mumbles that he never could seem to push the clutch in far enough...and this wasn't a revelation for him. From the moment we left the house, he was grinding gears and telling me that he just wasn't pushing the clutch in all the way. I really wanted to scream, "Push the freaking clutch all the way to the floor"...but I didn't. Finally, after what seemed like an eternity, he ground it into first gear...and then, he released the clutch too quickly and we lunged forward and stalled the engine...about a car length into the intersection. By now, I'm officially mortified...and again, it's all about these two old dudes out there in an equally old car in the middle of a fast moving, modern day freeway interchange. Because there were no sidewalks or shoulders that we could push the car on to and/or out of the way...we either had to get it started, or block traffic while trying to push it a block or more to a safe area. The two lanes beside us were moving okay, but the folks behind us were trapped until the two lanes beside us cleared and allowed them to go around us. Unlike me, Milford never panicked... he got the car restarted and ground back into first gear and we limped haltingly through the intersection as the overhead lights changed and once again, altered the directional flow of traffic.

Yes, we did eventually make it to Sears, and as my uncle had told me...more than once, "they" did know him down there. But to his surprise (not mine) they were unable to perform the requested tire service that we were seeking. However, being the full service company that they are, the mechanic did suggest a couple of websites that specialized in covered wagon wheels...I mean classic Model-A and Model-T Fords. Milford took it all in stride as we headed back to the house.

While Sears isn't everyone's store today, there was a time when "Sears, Roebuck and Company" was America's store for life's necessities. But again...that was yesteryear.

That evening I was telling his wife (she was at work during the day) about our daytrip when she enlightened me with some information that made the day's events even more entertaining. She went on to explain that none of his family members would ride with him anymore...not even in their ordinary everyday vehicles, much less the Model-A. She also told me that she had been trying to get his adult children together for a family intervention in an effort to talk him into giving up his driver's license. But his kids have been dragging their feet on what they know will be a heartbreaking, and probably contentious situation when they ask their father to give up a major portion of his independence.

I was already aware that Milford was forever asking Merlene (his wife), where various things were located and that he was telling the same stories over and over again. But he is still my favored Uncle Milford and as such, deserves my full attention when he shares his life experiences with me...over and over again. I know that each and every time he repeats a story, he's truly telling it for the first time...from his viewpoint. I listen and try to hear his words anew each time...even as I seek to reassure him that I'm listening and that I care. I know that by maintaining eye contact during his stories, he knows I'm interested in hearing what he has to say and that I value him as an individual. I understand his need to share his past...before *going home*.

I have recently come to realize that I occasionally repeat myself when sharing information with others. But make no mistake, I'm fully aware when I do not have my listener's full attention...so please, just tell me that I've already shared that knowledge and/or anecdote with you. Do not patronize me...because I will know (no matter my age).

I've already written much about how my uncle treasures the many items he continues to collect and hold on to from his early years. I know they represent the past, his life...and that he's just trying to hold on, even as he accepts the inevitable.

I also believe that one can *go home* before the physical departure actually takes place. A friend of mine who is shepherding her aging parents through the darkness of Alzheimer's disease wrote a very touching poem based on her day-to-day observations. I requested, and was graciously granted, permission to include the poem in my new book.

As my parents slide down the path of dementia I realize the value of "links to the past," material possessions that are kept for no other reason than to hold a memory.

Links To The Past

Why do some of us need the tangible, the physical?
To remember the day, the moment.
When you remove an item from your past,
The memory of the past may be released.
If you keep the item, each time you see it,
You will smile and remember that day.
But when dementia comes along,
Memories are fleeting.
Possessions help tether that memory,

Still wrapped around the brain.
Until dementia finally releases the line.
The rope floats in the water,
Down the stream, further and further.
Memories are gone, possessions are now meaningless.

Questions asked, again and again.
Confusion reigns on ponies high.
Memories that come and go,
Replaced by fog or innuendo.
Clouds of thought, moments of anger.
Things remembered, things forgotten.
Did you do this, did you do that? They ask.
Why must you keep telling me? I ask.
I'm not a child; I'm not a kid.
Don't treat me like I'm stupid.
I'll remember, I'll forget.
The "me" is still in here,
The one you love.
Don't treat me like a dummy.
It's not something I can control.
The pieces of me you know are still here.
Remember forever the person you knew,
As a child, a teenager, a young adult.
The one who held you when you were sad,
The parent who laughed at all of your bad jokes.
Remember for me, my entire life...
And pass on my wisdom,
Pass it on to everyone you know...
The soul of everything I am.

Claudia Van Gee

CHAPTER 14

I know that our ever-changing world is fast passing me by, I feel as though the train left the station without me... sometime ago, and I'm standing on the boarding platform watching as the caboose grows faint in the distance.

Americans differ today on when old age actually begins, but on average, they say 68. People under age 30 believe it begins at 60, while those 65 and older push the threshold to 74. Of all those surveyed, most said they wanted to live to about 89.

Getting older (sounds better than getting old) isn't as bad as people believe in terms of health, but isn't as good when it comes to lifestyle. While more than half of those under 65 think they will experience some memory loss when they're older, only one-quarter of people 65 and older say they are experiencing memory loss. Older folks are also reporting fewer instances than expected of problems such as serious illness, nor being able to drive, being less sexually active or depressed.

On the other hand, older adults end up having less leisure time than expected. While 87 percent of those under 65 think they'll have more time for hobbies and other interests in their old age, only 65 percent of older people report having it. Life at 65 and older also fell below expectations when it came to time with family, travel, having more financial security and less stress.

From my perspective (again), a great deal of the negative aspects (excluding health problems) that are coming to bear on the current generations' retirement plans are driven by their children and grandchildren. It's all too common to find adult children living at home...some with their own kids, and living pretty well too...because they don't always contribute monetarily...or otherwise, to the household. Grandparents are also caught in the middle as they are often called upon to raise a grandchild... or two, because of irresponsible parent(s). These same grandparents may then be forced to refinance a mortgage free home that had allowed them to retire in the first place. That money is then used to bail out their child, their adult children(s) and/or grandchildren...leaving the aging grandparents with a monthly mortgage payment and no discretionary money. The drivers for these co-habitation, state of affairs can be any number of issues ranging from drugs, lack of work ethic, social values, morality, lifestyle, relationships, and the biggie ...out of control, financial self-indulgence. Whatever the driver, money is always the answer...and the consumers will eventually drag his or her family deeper and deeper into that financial black hole that they've probably been digging for awhile.

So it should come as no surprise that today's generation gap is at its widest since the 1960s. But our current generation gap seems to be more tepid in nature than it was in the 1960s, when younger people built a defiant counter-culture in opposing the Vietnam War and demanding equal rights for women and minorities.

Today, it's more of an all-purpose, difference of opinion... generally, just a dissimilar set of moral values and character traits.

It just seems to me that the consuming desire of too many individuals is to deliberately plant their whole life in the hands of some other person. I would describe this method of searching for happiness as grossly immature. Development of character consists solely in moving toward self-sufficiency...but one must possess the desire and vision to see beyond today.

We've heard the disparaging observation when someone has been described as a "willy-nilly." We all have a different understanding of its definition, but we're pretty much correct because it's an all-encompassing affront. And for many of these individuals, the willy-nilly guidance system is often better than his or her immature, everyday judgment. It could also be said that without their willy-nilly method of sorting out life, they would have no direction at all.

So where am I going with this line of thought...and didn't I say, a chapter or so back, that I was going to get off our younger generation(s) case? Well, how 'bout I just dissect a couple of today's commonly accepted adages without pointing fingers?

The first one is, "Lighten up...don't take yourself so seriously, because no one else does." Well, if we don't take ourselves seriously, how can we expect others to take us seriously? I personally don't appreciate it when someone, jokingly or otherwise...suggests that I should lighten up. While life is a serious journey it can also provide the common sense traveler with a balanced passage...pleasurable and rewarding if managed with the seriousness it deserves. Continue to play the clown while making ill-advised decisions and choices and at some point in time, you will become the joke (in the minds of those around you) that you are projecting, and the joke will be on you. You will be seen as such...and not one to be trusted with serious responsibilities.

And the second one is, "Don't be so prideful...because pride can take you down the wrong roads." Yes, haughty, unmanaged and/or ill-directed pride can be a detriment in all areas of one's life...personal and career. But without pride we are without motivation; without motivation... we are without direction. Pride is a manageable...and renewable, human resource that drives the human soul. When I landed in California 50 years ago as a high school dropout, I had wandered into deep water...and was floundering in a sea of ignorance. But my survival mode pride would not accept failure as an elective lifestyle.

The people who prosper in this world are the individuals who get up everyday and look for the circumstances they desire, and if they can't find them...they create them. "In the final analysis, our only real freedom is the freedom to discipline ourselves."

Today's entitlement culture has lost the resilience and fortitude inherent in our earlier generations. They don't possess the mental toughness necessary to weather the inevitable storms of life.

One of Vince Lombardi's favorite subjects was head and heart...mental toughness. He believed that mental toughness was the single most important quality an individual should develop in themselves and the people around them. Mental toughness is the ability to hold on to your goals in the face of the pressure and stress of your current situation...whatever it might be. Mental toughness is the glue that can hold a family together when the heat is on, and help them persevere just a little longer, which in many cases is just long enough to outlast their crisis...and reach the turning point.

Lombardi's brand of mental toughness dated back to his college days at Fordham University where he was just an average player when compared to some of his more talented teammates. He played mainly because of his determination. He once played an entire game with a cut inside his mouth that required 30 stitches to close after the game. He said, "I can't exactly put my finger on what I learned during my playing days...because it was something intangible, a certain toughness... determination."

He schooled his players in the mental approach to football, telling them, "Hurt is in the mind," and he stressed that in order to win, they would have to disregard the small hurts and ignore the pressure.

In talking about mental toughness, he would emphasize the necessity of staying the course even when things would go wrong. He talked about using failure as motivation to come back stronger than before. He once said, "Sometimes it's good to have an obstacle to overcome, whether in football or everyday life." When things go bad, we usually rise to the occasion...we learn perseverance by persevering.

Mental toughness is the ability to be at your best at all times, regardless of the circumstances. It's easy to do well when there's no stress, but how many of us can be poised when the pressure is on? Mental toughness is constancy of purpose; it is focus and emotional control. Mental toughness is not rigidity in the face of adversity; it is stability and poise in the face of challenge. Mental toughness is seeking out the pressure that can't be avoided anyway and being energized by it. It's not just the ability to survive a mistake or failure; it's the ability to come back stronger from failure.

Mental toughness isn't inherent. It's not something we're born with. It is learned just like every other quality that is required to rise above mediocrity.

My son, Lance, is an excellent example of a Lombardi prototype. As an athlete he never gave up on a game as long as there was still time on the clock...until that final horn sounded and proved him wrong, he always believed a victory was obtainable. I also know that more than once or twice, he played hurt and/or sick when he should have stayed at home. Because he was always a key player for whatever team he was on, he felt a responsibility to be there for the team.

San Jose State (a Division I College) gave him a football scholarship in spite of scouting reports with footnotes indicating that he was a Division I player with Division II speed. But those same reports were supportive of his knowledge of the game, his competitive nature and how he was able to anticipate his opponent's game plan. He was also a coach and cheerleader on the field where he led by example.

And as most of you know (from my earlier books) he went on to become a head coach himself, and later the athletic director at a large high school here in Orange County.

CHAPTER 15

Driving through the hours I found that my solitude allowed my mind to drift more seamlessly back to my beginnings. While many things were resurrected... the good, the bad and a lot of gray area in-between... some clear and detailed, others remaining murky and questionable...and rightfully so. We know, from my first book, what propelled me out into the bigger world, but were there underlying drivers that I was oblivious to? Why do some remain home while others leave...only to search for the path back, as their lives wind down? And why do we say, you can never go home...?

I've heard it said, "In fantasy and myth, homecoming is a dramatic event...bands play, the fatted calf is killed, a banquet is prepared, and there is rejoicing that the prodigal has returned. But the reality is that exile is most commonly ended gradually, with no dramatic external events to mark its passing. The haze in the air evaporates and the world comes into focus, seeking gives way to finding, anxiety to satisfaction. Everything has changed...yet nothing has changed."

On my earlier road trip (before this book was conceived) my first goal was to get through Arizona and New Mexico as quickly as possible...like drive straight through. Well, that didn't happen, but after an abbreviated, 3:30 AM, Motel-6 stop in Tucumcari, New Mexico, I was in the vicinity of Oklahoma City by noon the next day. After a short visit with some distant relatives on the Warren side of the family (Milford's suggestion), I headed south toward Texas. But even before I left California, the possibility of locating a long-ago friend had been an abstract thought. And I say abstract because it had been almost 50 years since I had seen him and I could only remember that he lived in a small Podunk-like, Oklahoma, rural community. So what were the odds? I couldn't recall the name of the little town...and even if I could, would he still be living there...or would he still be living at all?

But by now, I've pretty much put the thought of locating my old buddy to rest as I'm motoring south, on Interstate 35, about a hundred miles (give or take) from the Texas border. I'm taking in the Oklahoma landscape and minding its traffic "suggestions" when out of the corner of my eye, I saw an official interstate road sign informing me that the next exit would take me to Wynnewood, Oklahoma. Not Podunk, but Wynnewood...and that's when the light came on..."that's the name of the town!" But I still didn't have an address or a phone number to determine the status of the other two variables.

I swung into a local Holiday Inn and by blending in with the paying clientele, I was able to utilize one of their courtesy computers and found a number for a Donald Whitaker on the Internet. But when I called it...I was informed that it was no longer in service. I then called information and was given a different number for a Donald Whitaker. A man answered my call, but when I announced who I was he went silent for a moment before asking me, "So who are you calling." I replied that I was trying to locate an old friend named, Donald Whitaker. He then came back with, "I'm Donald Whitaker, but I don't think we know each other." I was caught off guard by his statement, but before I could respond to him he came back with a reflective-like after-thought. "Richard Neal...are you Donald's ex-brother-in-law?" I was even more confused now as I answered in the affirmative before continuing with our question and answer game. I then asked him, "But didn't you just tell me that you're Donald Whitaker?" He then countered (with a straight face, I'm sure) by saying, "I'm Donald Joe Whitaker and you're probably looking for my cousin, Donald Gene Whitaker." He then proceeded to give me his cousin's phone number...true story!

After thanking Donald Joe and making a call for directions to Donald Gene, I headed over to my friend's place for a catch-up visit with him, his wife Laquieta, and their family. Everyone seemed to remember me; but of course Don did have time to do some coaching before my arrival.

While I was there, I was given a personal tour of "WHITAKER'S WINERY (located in the spare bedroom)," Wynnewood, Oklahoma. I was also given a complimentary bottle of his "STRAWBERRY THRILL" which I viewed as an attempt to imitate Fats Domino's 50s hit, Blueberry Hill...where he sang about finding his "thrill on Blueberry Hill."

But the high point of our reunion was toward the end of our visit when he brought out...in his words, some pictures from our past. The two photographs he handed me blew me away because, even though I was prominent in both depictions, I had/have no memory of them being taken. However, the fact remains that we were in Tijuana, "Old Mexico," sometime during the year of 1960. We know this because in the background of one of the pictures, there is some promotional signage that documented the date and location. Sue (my first wife) and I were there with Donald and Jo (Sue's younger sister) to witness and support their wedding. Their marriage didn't survive for long, falling apart about the same time that Sue and I began drifting apart. As I've already indicated, my recall on all of this is a little skewed (okay, so I don't have clue) but it seems that after the break-ups...and over differing time periods, we all just kinda scattered. Both girls ending up back in Hope, Donald in Oklahoma and I made a life in California.

So for Don and I, everything has changed...yet nothing has changed.

My friend, Jerry, died over 10 years ago, and everything has changed...yet nothing has changed. I still think of him and remember our special friendship and the crazy things we did...usually things we shouldn't have done. We even joked about that old proverb that suggested, if you think an action is wrong, you probably shouldn't be doing it...but we did it anyway!

My high school friend, Max, died about nine years ago and everything has changed, yet nothing has changed because he's still my friend and I still remember our time together...we were the "Hoods."

My high school friend, Kenneth, lost his daughter to Lou Gehrig's Disease late last year (2008) leaving the care of her three children to Kenneth and his wife, Billie. A year earlier, Kenneth had lost a kidney to cancer but everyone believed his prognosis was good. In spite of his doctor's encouraging reports, in January 2008, Kenneth was found to have developed bone cancer in his hip and lung cancer. I will be visiting with him at some point during this road trip. Again I can say that everything has changed...but how can I rationalize that nothing has changed?

From my perspective, a part of it's about that spiritual... soul affecting, personal relationship between people who have truly connected and care deeply about each other. That should never change; it's about the intangibles. But how can I contend that nothing has changed in the dynamics of their real-world, physical existence? There will of course be questions and decisions to deal with, like who will be raising the children and whether or not his wife will be able to handle the situation on her own... given her age. Those issues will remain unchanged (nothing has changed) and challenging, and they will absolutely require someone's attention...because life will continue unabated. Those concerns will not change nor go-a-way...they must, and will be addressed, whether by Kenneth and Billie...or someone else.

Whenever he passes, his physical presence will most certainly be missed, but his essence...his spirit, will be there within each and every member of his family, I have no doubt. I know that I will always remember my friend, Kenneth.

I also located Billy, another friend from high school that I hadn't been in touch with for over 35 years. In high school, Billy was a part-time Hood...kinda in and out, not exactly a paying member, but he was one of us. He was a nice looking guy with a rebel air about him, but his real claim to fame was the persistent rumor around school that he was maintaining a sexual relationship with one of our English teachers. I can't recall him being boastful about it or even privately bringing the subject up within our group, but the gossip was out there and true or false...it elevated him (among the guys) to a celebrity-like status.

The timeframe is somewhat distorted, but it seems that we both left Hope early. I headed off to California and Billy joined a branch of the military. Approximately 15 years later, I learned from his father (a lifelong resident of Hope) that Billy was stationed in San Francisco, California. My family (wife and kids) subsequently paid a visit (approximately 1974) to him and his family at the Presidio of San Francisco, which before its closure in 1989 was the oldest continuously operating military base in the country.

While in Hope, on the first leg of my *going home* road trip, I was put in touch with Billy by my resident historian (another story), Jessie Tullis. I first spoke with Billy on the phone and later drove out to his place at the edge of town, for a visit. I already knew from our phone conversation that he wasn't in the best of health, that he was living on government disability and that he was sharing a place with his father...but it would be worse than I expected.

Their modest, singlewide, mobile home was near the entrance to the trailer park, just off old Highway 67. I rang the doorbell and waited...they were expecting me so I was a little surprised at their delay in coming to the door. But just as I was about to push that button again, the door slowly cracked open...and it was Billy. I was immediately made aware of his hindrance, he had been pushing and shuffling along with one of those four-legged, wrap-a-round walkers on his way from his large recliner to the front door. My first thought(s) were a couple of opposing emotions...physically Billy moved and looked as though his life was over, but he was well groomed, he had a smile on his face and was still a good-looking man. His father, who coincidentally sold me my first two cars back in the 50s, slowly rose from his large recliner, shook my hand and insisted that I take his chair as he settled down on the couch. Billy, in the mean time, was repositioning himself back in his comfort zone.

As I was about to take my seat, I couldn't help but notice that a large portion of the kitchen counter looked like a dedicated storage area for at least 30, and perhaps more, prescription bottles of all shapes, sizes and colors. I jokingly quizzed Billy about the drugstore in the kitchen and he came back with his own humorous retort. He replied that it was about a 50 – 50 split between his and his father's medications. He added that he sometimes wonders who's taking what...with all the prescriptions bearing the same last name, and his dad's obsession about taking medication...his or mine. He was just kidding of course...I think. He also mentioned that just keeping up with the timing of each of their medications was enough to keep them occupied all day...everyday.

At some point in his life (I didn't request details) Billy got into alcohol and gambling, and over time...they became his life. His dad who also enjoyed a little imbibing and gaming was drawn into his son's addictions and was often called upon to rescue Billy from aggressive bookies demanding payment for his gambling debts. On one occasion when his bookie came after him for money owed, Billy offered his car as payment, but the collector said, "I don't want your car...I got a yard full of cars from people just like you, I want my money." It seems that his father bailed him out many times, even borrowing from his family to pay Billy's markers. But eventually, even they said, "Enough is enough."

Before I departed, I couldn't resist asking Billy the biggest question of all..."So tell me, were you really having an affair with one of our high school English teachers?" He quickly came back with an exaggerated, indignant response, "No, that's totally untrue Richard...it was the History teacher!"

Billy's lifestyle consumed everything...his personal health, his financial health, but more importantly...even his family was forced to abandon him. And with that forfeiture...I believe his peace of mind was profoundly compromised...far beyond any of the above listed losses. I saw so much of my son (Landon) in my friend, Billy. I just pray it's not a foretelling premonition...

The time we spent catching up was time well spent for me; their stories validated what I've always believed. "First we form habits, then they form us. Conquer your bad habits, or they'll eventually conquer you."

Yes, everything has changed, in that we're in different places...mentally, spiritually, physically and financially. But more importantly, the passing of time and the realities of the real world have changed our expectation of life. We'll all pay a toll...some more than others, for a no-guarantee journey with random, unannounced... but mandatory departures along the way. Our sojourns are brief at best...and with far too many premature departures, the knowledge of unrealized dreams and aspirations can unknowingly be buried with the dreamer. And once again, everything has changed; yet nothing has changed.

CHAPTER 16

On my return to Hope, my first two contacts will be Jessie Tullis and John Smith, neither of whom I knew before my earlier visit. I became good friends with them during my stay back in February and March. While our paths crossed independently of each other, remarkable circumstances played out and allowed me to meet each of these men, but they are not acquainted with each other. They enthusiastically embraced my mission and both became instrumental in my quest for those long-ago friends and acquaintances.

Jessie and I became buddies, in part, because I'm a terrible speller. As I entered the city limits and headed on down W 3rd, I saw the J & E Motor Co signage over the small used car lot. My first thought was that Billy's dad, after all these years, still owned the business where I purchased my used cars as a teenager. I pulled into the lot and found a friendly individual who introduced himself as Jessie. I told him my name and shared my thoughts about the lot still being owned by my friend's father (J. B. Ingram). Jessie tactfully explained that my erroneous assumption, that Ingram was spelled with an E...not an I, was understandable given my apparent early training in phonics, but that he had owned the place for sometime, having purchased it from the man I was seeking.

I met and befriended John while staying at the Holiday Express where he worked part-time. We crossed paths one day in the hallway, and because he appeared to be about my age...I asked him, "Are you James?" Understandably, he looked perplexed as he replied that he was not. As I had with Jessie, I went on to tell John who I was and explain that I was born there but had left 50 years earlier. I also enlightened him about my motivation for initiating such an off-the-wall inquiry.

A few chapters back I wrote about some lingering details that I'm hoping to put to rest in this book. The first, you already know about...finding a biological son that I've never met. The second one began over 50 years ago as a teenager growing up in Arkansas. I brought it to life in my first book and now I'm hoping to lay it to rest...dead or alive. And like the first search, the trail is cold and lacking vital information such as, exact age and a full name. James and I were friends back in the 50s when it wasn't "politically correct," and we were as conspicuous as black and white. I only knew (or remember) James by his first name and a nickname..."Snowball." James was approximately my age and we were both physically gifted...six-foot tall and slender. In retrospect...we were both, apparently...also colorblind.

During my first stay in Hope, my casual search style yielded a surprising number of informational nuggets. My casual search style was that if you looked 50 or older, seemed halfway friendly and made eye contact with me, we were going to talk. In addition to the numerous classmates that I spoke with, I encountered several individuals who only knew of me, but they knew my younger siblings. One fellow told me that he had had a crush on my sister in high school...he also knew that she and our brother had both passed early. That conversation only took place because in Small Town, America, outsiders stand out from the locals. They just know you're an out-of-towner...it's kinda spooky. We had made eye contact during lunch and on his way out, he just casually stopped by my table to inquire about where I was from. I told him who I was and that I was from Hope...50 years ago. That's when he told me about knowing my sister and brother, and gave me his name, David Porterfield.

In my search for James, I spoke with many residents on both sides of that old black and white dividing line, but the lack of a complete name was very problematic. While I wasn't able to find James or nail down his current whereabouts (dead or alive), I was encouraged by the number of folks willing to talk about the possibilities. I received only one sarcastic reply to my many inquiries, and it was from a classmate who shall remain nameless. He said, "Oh, we probably hung him years ago." Of course he was kidding, but our words resonate from within...we are what we say, even when we say we were just kidding. There's an old adage that states: We can cut our own throat with a sharp tongue.

As I've said before, my little hometown (to my knowledge) has never experienced the overtly, physical, hostility of racism, but the subtleties spoke loud and clear. I still believe (in my heart) that the majority of the whites (in my town) viewed the bulk of the blacks as good, decent people; I also believe most of the blacks felt the same about most of the whites. I have to wonder if it wasn't just a continuum of the bond that was forged during slavery, with both sides struggling with separating themselves from their past...that co-dependency relationship. There was a deep-seated psychological mindset where each side had its own set of ingrained parameters that directed their lives without questioning the moral correctness of it all. I'm not suggesting that it was right...I'm only saying that "that's just the way it was"...back then.

During this leg of my journey, I will be talking with people of both colors in an effort to get below the superficial surface of what I've already observed...that racially, the South has turned the corner. I'll have no trouble finding whites willing to share their true feelings, and while I was there, a few months back...I developed trustworthy bonds with several African-Americans who I'm sure will be willing to provide me with an opposing point of view... the black community's.

Race and religion have always...and will continue to drive wedges between men. It is the innate nature of mankind to generally distrust those we view as different from ourselves. And, as if that's not enough, we have our modern-day agitators fueling the fire to keep the pot boiling...for their personal, self-serving agenda.

We're all aware of the reoccurring phenomenon of Jackson and/or Sharpton materializing (Johnny on the spot) at all high profile incidents where blacks and whites conflict. They'll also show up at situations that, in many cases, were moving toward resolution before their arrival. And...they somehow always manage to have the media in tow, with cameras rolling.

Does anyone truly believe they're (including the media) out there in the best interest of this person who's claiming discrimination and/or racism? They're out there because it's their job to keep these issues (true or perceived) front and center. Without continuous race allegations, Jackson and Sharpton's livelihoods could be jeopardized. Another thing that you may not have noticed is that they never seem to return to the scene of the crime after the facts are made public and the truth has become irrelevant. They accomplished their mission, the damage was done, everyone saw them (on television) spewing out unsupported accusations with little to no rebut...because the would-be defenders were appropriately, waiting for all the facts to rise to the surface. But the attackers just want to get their slanted version out to the public before the real story hits the streets. They know that by the time an investigation is conducted and the truth comes out, the public will have already moved on to the next charade...and that only their irresponsible assertions will be remembered.

I strongly believe that the above actions play against society's continuing efforts to improve race relations. I know that from my perspective and others that I've spoken with, there is building resentment (among whites) to Jackson and Sharpton's on going, dog-and-pony shows. And I have wondered if this method of perpetuating racism and entitlement isn't wearing a little thin with the rank and file blacks also...perhaps even a little embarrassing at times. I have no doubt that the majority of blacks are hard working, responsible folks and when they see the opportunists out there working the system...they see it as a reflection of them as a whole. I feel the same way when I see someone of my race representing us in a despicable or degrading way...and I'm not referring to Bubba because he just doesn't know any better. Remember the Jerry Springer Show? It always seemed to me that perhaps he was discriminating because he almost always had our white-trailer-trash folks on his show, but neither Jackson nor Sharpton ever showed up with the media.

Enough of that...what we need is more of Thomas Sowell and Bill Cosby's "take" on life. Both, like me, are old-school conservatives and share my perspective on the decline of community standards, personal values, personal responsibility and accountability, and just a general lack of good old common sense in today's generation(s). It's not so much about the color of one's skin, as it is about his or her "take" on life.

Reactions to Bill Cosby's recent criticisms of some counterproductive ghetto behavior patterns ranged from applause from many in the black audience, to a cheap attack from white liberal Barbara Ehrenreich in the New York Times. "Billionaire bashes poor blacks" is the way she put it.

Over the years, Bill Cosby has poured enough of his efforts and money into advancing blacks that he does not need any lessons from Barbara Ehrenreich on how to help his own people. Her attempt to pose as a friend and defender of blacks has implications that reach far beyond her self-serving agenda.

According to Ms. Ehrenreich, "it's so 1985 to beat up on the poor blacks." Among her other radical chic comments was, "it must be fun to beat up on people too young and too poor to fight back or the elderly rich wouldn't do it."

This is just one of innumerable ways that the political left evades criticisms...whether regarding young thugs, schoolteachers or anyone else, by simply calling the criticism "bashing" and thereby shifting the focus to the supposedly bad motives of those who criticize.

Criticism is part of the price for progress. Economics professor Walter Williams has said that a turning point in his education, and his life...came when a schoolteacher in the Philadelphia ghetto chewed him out for wasting his abilities on adolescent nonsense. The criticism hurt...but there was no Barbara Ehrenreich around to defend him. So he turned his life around.

But today, how many white schoolteachers are going to chew out some ghetto youth? How many white college students are going to tell a black roommate to stop goofing off?

In today's climate, too many teachers think they are doing black students a favor by feeding them grievances from the past and telling them how they are oppressed in the present, and how their future is blocked by white racism. These are the kinds of friends who do more damage than one's enemies.

Why endure all the hard work, self-discipline and self-denial that a first-rate education requires if "The Man" is going to stop you from getting anywhere anyway? People who have been pushing this line for years are now suddenly surprised and dismayed to discover that many black students across the country regard academic striving as "acting white."

Many young blacks likewise regard speaking correct English, or even observing the rules of polite society, as "acting white." White liberals often cheer them on in their self-destructive behavior or at least "understand" and defend them.

Many white liberals have in effect, adopted blacks as mascots. Mascots serve to symbolize something for others, but the actual well being of the mascot himself is seldom a major concern. The left has long used Blacks to indict America's society.

People like Barbara Ehrenreich get their jollies saying clever things to needle America's society, whether on race or other issues. The actual consequences of their liberal vision for blacks get remarkably little attention.

So what if the social pathologies in the black community grew far worse after liberal doctrines became government policies in the 1960s? The vision is what matters to the left...and of course the opportunities it presents for them to be clever with words.

Civil rights used to be about treating everyone the same. But today some people are so used to special treatment that equal treatment is often considered to be discrimination.

"The difference between a successful person and others is not a lack of strength, nor a lack of knowledge, but rather a lack of will."

CHAPTER 17

Rural America has almost always run under the speed limits while the big cities have always exceeded those same speed limits. But today, with our new normlessness, there doesn't seem to be any recognized...or acknowledged limits on speed or anything else.

I was having lunch with some friends in Hope and was surprised as I listened to them talking about how everyone was in such a big hurry. How they seemed agitated and/or hostile and oblivious to how their actions were affecting those surrounding them.

I said, "If you guys think your locals are aggressive, agitated and rude, then you don't wanna come to Orange County. We have the most up-tight, aggressive, get-out-of-my-way motorists and pedestrians that you can imagine."

But yes, even rural America has been drawn into our new up-tempo society; they haven't reached warp speed yet (like O.C. and L.A.), but they're definitely picking up speed. And as in the metropolitan areas this accelerated lifestyle is driven by various intangibles, but lack of proper prioritization, self-facilitating organization and procrastination are the biggest drivers. Couple all that with today's "me first" generation racing around town trying to catch-up with their out-of-control lives... which are days ahead of them, and you have a lot of impatient emotions festering out there on our highways and byways.

Life has no guarantee and by its very nature, will subject us to many of its ironies. My friend Kenneth, like myself, is an old school, do the right thing and play by the rules dinosaur that worked hard at keeping his life in order and on track...but even when one does all the right things, there are no assurances.

One of the first stops on my road trip was down to Shongaloo, Louisiana, to visit Kenneth. I arrived around noon (a pre-agreed upon time) and Billie greeted me at the door before advising Kenneth that I had arrived... he was resting in bed after having taken some pain medication. He soon joined us in the living room wearing a t-shirt and sweatpants and made his way to the big recliner where he stayed for the next three hours. He talked continuously during that time, but never a word of negativity. During the course of our visit he received numerous calls from well-wishers and two longtime friends dropped by.

Their three grandkids (seven, nine and eleven) that they have adopted, because their father, like too many today, typifies today's growing trend of fathers walking away and leaving a single mother, are now living with Kenneth and Billie. The five of them are living in a 45-year-old, singlewide mobile home...with two bedrooms and one bath, with plumbing problems. The current plan is to sell the daughter's vacant singlewide mobile home, their aging home (just for the cost of hauling it away) and bring in a new modular home for the family. The community has gathered round with offers to do the grading for the modular and all the electrical hook-ups for free. A website was built to bring their situation to light and fundraisers were organized as their friends and neighbors pulled together. It all brought back memories of yesteryear when we cared about each other.

Due to visitors coming and going, I didn't get the opportunity to talk with Kenneth privately; but I did have a private...albeit brief, enlightening conversation with his wife. I of course asked about the battle, and she was up-front regarding the cancer spreading and that his treatment program had become ineffective. But when I asked about his long-term prognosis, she, understandably, did not want to say...she just said, "I can't talk about it."

I also asked how the kids were taking the loss of their mother and now...the possibility of losing their grandfather (although I suspect this is all outside their realm of comprehension and it will be years before the affects will manifest themselves). She replied that they seem fine except for the middle child who hugs her a lot and tells her that he loves her.

But the really telling question and answer was when I asked her about dealing with a teenage daughter in a couple of years and two boys following close behind. Her plaintive response spoke volumes about Kenneth's longevity. She said, "Yes, I understand the difficulties of raising teenagers in today's world...and I'll be 70 when she turns 13." She didn't say they would be 70...she said

131

she would be 70. What I heard was that Kenneth would not be there to help her.

The irony here is that my friend had done all the right things, but in the end he has lost control of his life at the most crucial time...when his family needs him the most, and through no fault of his own.

I didn't get what I'm about to write from Kenneth himself or his wife Billie, but I know exactly what his concerns and fears are wrapped around. I know because we're both "men's men" and as such, principles mean everything to us. He's not afraid of dying, but his pride and self-worth are taking a beating. He has a responsibility to his family (that he loves dearly) and he's leaving them behind in a situation that they are ill prepared to handle on their own. Cancer may be taking his life, but the thought of leaving his family alone in their most dire situation is taking his soul.

After three hours, I said good-bye to my friend and headed back to Hope, wondering if I had actually said good-bye... for the last time.

Upon arriving back in Hope, I pulled into Neighbors' Gas and Mini-Mart to fill my gas tank. As I'm finishing up I notice a city vehicle pulling into a space in front of the store and a black man (approximately my age) getting out of the truck. Of course you know where my thoughts are going...I followed him into the mini-mart and after he purchased his beverage, I approached him with my patented, if not subtle, question..."Are you James?" After an awkward pause he replied, "No I'm not...why do you ask?" I told him who I was and that I had lived there 50 years ago and that I was searching for an old friend who I only knew by his first name...James. I added that because he fit my generic profile (black, close to my age and living in Hope), I was compelled to ask...or I would always wonder.

As he indulged me, and not wanting to lose his attention, I quickly went on to elaborate about my search for a long-ago friend. I explained how we hung out together and that he attended Yerger High School (all black at the time) and I attended Hope High School (all white). His response was very encouraging as he told me his name was Calvin Ware, that he was 68 (a year older than me) and that he had also attended Yerger High School. But he was struggling with the fact that we only had a first name to work with. I then mentioned that James had a very interesting nickname as a teenager and that if it stuck with him, it would be memorable. I still had his interest as I said, "His nickname was Snowball." I immediately saw a light come on in his eyes as he, with a monotone, matter-a-fact voice, said, "James 'Snowball' Jones." I, of course, was very excited that my grassroots hunt was finally paying off. I say grassroots because that was my only avenue without a last name, birth year and/or death year. I had already run the various on-line searches for vital records (local and state), but the first three questions on every site asked for a last name, birth date and death date if deceased...case closed.

As we talked he informed me that James had indeed been killed in a car crash years earlier. I had heard this possibility when I was in Hope back in the spring, but no one could say for sure because (as I'm now learning) it happened so very long ago. Calvin did not know the date of the accident, but advised me that he often ran into James' brother around town and would get his phone number for me...and he did. He also opened the door for the conversation before I phoned.

I called Bobby Lee (James' half-brother), and he was very helpful and cooperative...he even gave me their sister's phone number for questions that he didn't have answers for or was unsure of. Bobby told me he was driving the car that James was killed in...when they crashed into a concrete bridge abutment. It seems that James always preferred the front passenger seat (which took the brunt of the impact as the car slammed into the concrete) and because of that preference, he was the only one of five who perished in the accident. And I can relate to James' seat selection; as a teenager, if I wasn't driving...I always wanted to be riding "shotgun." Bobby said the crash was caused by a problem with the steering column.

After speaking with Bobby Lee, I placed a call to his sister Lucy, for additional information (mostly dates) pertaining to James' abbreviated life. Lucy, (James' younger sister) was also very helpful...even calling another relative for the exact date of James' death. She then gave me directions to the cemetery and the general location of his resting place within. Just before I thanked her and said good-bye, Lucy reminisced that James just had a birthday a few days earlier. "He would have been 71 this past July 31, 2009," she said.

James died at 25 years of age and never married or had children. He had always worked...beginning back when he worked nights (as a teenager) busing tables at the Diamond Café at the corner of Main Street and Highway 67. If you read my first book, you already know that's where we met.

James Edward Jones
Born: July 31, 1938
Died: April 6, 1963
Scott Memorial Cemetery

It felt strange to stand at the foot of his grave...about 52 years after we went our separate ways. I wondered if he ever thought about me...but I think probably not, we're all too busy early in life to reflect much on our past. It's only later in life that we appreciate and/or value the past and James...unfortunately, didn't live long enough to experience the *going home* phase of life.

There are things that we don't want to happen, but have to accept. There are things we don't want to know, but have to learn. And there are people we can't live without, but we have to let them go.

CHAPTER 18

The next morning I headed out toward the crossroads...
and another cemetery. My Mother is buried in the
Westmoreland Cemetery, and as I did on my earlier trip
back there, I was going out to visit with her for a while.
The route out of town was a small, secondary, two-way
traffic road disappearing into the countryside. Several
miles out I arrived at the crossroads where I turned
left onto an even smaller, rural side-road...but still two-
way traffic. I had driven only two or three miles when
I saw the Westmoreland Cemetery sign ahead; where I
made a right-hand turn onto a one-way, dirt, tree-lined
lane leading to a clearing in a wooded area about a 100
yards off the road. I pulled up to the entrance, got out
of my car, opened the swinging wire and aluminum gate
and drove my car inside. It's a small, private graveyard
that's maintained (very nicely) by friends and relatives.
The graves date from very current to as far back as
the 1700s. There is also a fence separating the Whites
from the Blacks and an additional entry for the Black
section. Both sides are well kept and share the beauty

and tranquility of the backdrop. One side of the tree-surrounded, garden-like oasis is wide open...like a picture window with a panoramic view of the colorful, springtime meadowland just below, on the sloping landscape...for those residing there.

As I had numerous times before, I made my way to the area where my Mother rested along side Elvin, Kay and their father...all together. It had never occurred to me before, but as I stood there looking down at the grouping...the picture was developing very clearly. They were a complete family structure, in life and in death. It was my Mother, but not my family foundation. I did not know my father and he has no physical resting place because his grave was desecrated and all corporeal traces disappeared in the interest of greed. And when I pass, I will be cremated and my ashes scattered at sea or to the prevailing winds in the mountains somewhere, and with no identifiable resting place...belonging no where, as always. All the above just skews my journey home...it seems, to me, that my voyage is uncertain at best.

I know that you would say, "But Richard, you have your own family unit...your sons and your daughter." And I would agree that I have my own family base, but it's not my generation...it belongs to my children. For me, there is a gap here...a missing link that will never be solidified.

I really didn't intend to get into this so deeply...and certainly didn't plan on dwelling on it, but it just keeps coming. A side benefit...or detriment (depending on one's point of view), of a long road trip alone, is that you have a lot of time with yourself...therapeutic time.

Driving through the vast emptiness of Arizona and New Mexico can become a lonely voyage in and of itself, and the feelings of isolation only exacerbate the situation. In that oneness, I found it easy to look back and examine my past...the whys and why-nots. And of course those classic country songs (about the realities of the real world) playing on the radio just took me back, to another time...another place. I would be the first to admit that we become more emotional as we move further down this *going home* path...heck, I almost cry over the weather forecast sometimes.

I want to preface this next segment with the fact that life has been good to me in the tangible sense...and that this should not be viewed as a pity party. But because I've never been this old before...I don't know if conceivably, what I'm about to share is more common than I realize. Perhaps it's a part of a natural progression as we accept and anticipate..."calling it a day."

I sense that these feelings of indescribable sadness have always been with me, but with the passing years they have slowly ascended closer and closer to the surface. There were times during my extended road trips that I felt as lonely as the beggar living on the street, with his disappearing dreams of yesterday. I also know, and accept, that I've always been a part of the problem. It seems that I'm always leaving, unable...or unwilling, to give enough. But even with my wanderlust, I stayed too long once or twice...and it hurt.

Life turns...on lessons learned.

While I found my friend, James, I wasn't so fortunate in my quest for my illegitimate son. Like James, I merely had a first name, Tyler, (which I only learned on this trip) and an approximate age to search with. It appears that he may have lived with his grandparents for a time (duration unknown) and that they lived behind Garland

Elementary School in Hope. It's also unknown which grandparents...his mother's parents or the adopting father's parents. But since she (his mother) came to Hope to live with her sister and brother-in-law after going through a divorce in Tennessee...and my grapevine source (my daughter, Rhonda) remembers her mother (Sue), years ago, referring to the adopting father by his full name, I would guess that he was a local resident. Rhonda has been unable to recall his name and to this point, Rhonda's mother has been less than helpful to me in my endeavor. Why...? I have my thoughts, but her reasoning is irrelevant and unimportant to the bigger issue here.

At the beginning of this book, as we started down this road, I suggested that he knows my full name and could easily find me...if he were ready. Being in his mid-forties, I doubt that he's yet burdened by our innate biological need and/or desire to *go home*, as in reconnecting with one's past. I believe that yearning is instilled in us at inception, but only fully manifests itself during the autumn of our lives. I would expect that at some point, down the road, Tyler, will reach out...not for a father, but just to acknowledge each other's existence and the common bond that connects us.

Hopefully before it's too late...

Blood may be thicker than water, but do biological genetic ties of kinship really matter that much in our modern world? These thoughts come to mind as Americans become drawn into the media watch of tragic custody struggles by the likes of Jessica McClure, a toddler who was rescued after she fell down a well in Midland, Texas in 1987. Anna Schmidt, also known as Jessica DeBoer, a child who was the subject of a well-publicized custody battle in Michigan and Iowa in the early 1990s.

When the conflicting claims of biological versus social parents clash, what values are in dispute?

I would suggest we're still a traditional, conservative society that tries to decide these cases based on what we're used to. We're used to biological parents. The implication is that to value biological kinship is to display a retrograde allegiance to the primitive and proprietary norms of our past...and a patriarchal past at that.

In the anti-biological perspective, truly meaningful human relationships are formed not by sharing genetic ties but by willed and autonomous consent. The highest human capacity is the rational ability to use symbols, to make promises, and to make conscious moral commitments. After all, as everyone recognizes, the culturally created bonds of marriage, adoption, ideological and religious communities can be as robust and intense as any genetic familial bond. So why make such a big deal of the biological connection in reproduction?

Well yes, but it is well to remember that individual human beings can create psychosocial, consensual bonds and autonomous commitments only because they have been genetically selected to inherit the innate brainpower and emotional capacity to produce family loyalties and long-term, caretaker characteristics. Moreover, these freely willed relationships of informed consent tend to become symbolized by images and metaphors derived from genetic ties. Believers are united in "one family" as "children of God" and live as "brothers and sisters" in the Lord.

Mother, father, sister, brother, daughter and son...human beings cherish their blood kin for many reasons that have nothing to do with patriarchy, property rights, or the inertia of custom. The biological links in a family create powerful bonds because they are particular, specific, and most important, irreversible. While one can divorce a spouse, the genetic tie between parent and child or between siblings can never be undone. Am I my brother's keeper? Yes, forever.

Moreover, genetic ties can be extended over time and space; they exist despite physical distance or the absence of daily encounters. Brothers, sisters, aunts, uncles, and cousins remain one's relatives no matter how far away they live. Even the dead exert influence.

Yes, biological relatives are irreversibly our own particular kin and we are stuck with them. But then they are stuck with us as well. You don't earn or achieve your status as a family member; you're born into the fold. These ties of blood kinship produce moral responsibilities that no one contracts for. Family obligations exist prior to other freely chosen allegiances or promises. We are born into earth's ecosystem without informed consent yet have a moral responsibility to take care of our environment now and for future generations.

When, in turn, we biologically engender a child with a partner, the two parents are equally invested and morally responsible for the child. At the same time, two different family lineages are united and new, extended bonds of biological kinship are created. Each child has two sets of kin to act as backups and additional resources for nurturing and helpful launching into the community. And the social capital provided by biological kin extends through adulthood and into old age. After one's spouse, friends, colleagues and comrades have died and left them behind and alone...they are still a part of their extended family. Whether sick, disabled and/or senile, they are still a family member and as such will be taken care of without question...because they are biological family elements. There's just an unspoken responsibility that binds.

In fact, our immersion in biological kinship prepares us for old age and strengthens the obligations that we owe to the old. In the mirror I see my face turning into my father's face with the same wrinkles and deep shadows, while my body slowly begins to resemble his as he advanced into old age. Having loved these physical bodies I can better come to terms with my aging body. The physical likeness, which is so undeniable, reminds me that these particulars will be passed on to my sons and daughter. In genetics, or pertaining to those generations following the initial (parental) generation...obligations cannot be denied. Through my aging parents I begin to empathize with other old people, to feel empathy in relation to another person.

As for our children, the genetic tie also becomes more important as they age. We value our growing children not as personal property or as personal achievements, but partly because they are biologically like us, like one's spouse, and like our other family members. My genes are shared with my parents and siblings, and my biological child shares in these family resemblances. Biological similarities make it easier for one to understand and be attuned to a harmonious or responsive relationship...a child of my flesh, akin to me and mine.

The biological link to children is particularly supportive to parents in the crisis time of adolescence. In this trying period of separating and achieving independence, many members of a family might choose to divorce (if not murder) each other if they could. The irreversible biological bond helps hold parents to their task; one's parental authority is augmented when the parent-child tie is irreversibly "just the way it is," courtesy of nature's genetic throw, with no undoing possible. Like it or not, we're all in this family together.

When one's children become adults and move out into their grown-up lives, the family's daily encounters and mutual exchanges lessen. But kinship ties, despite many difficulties, can still operate from a distance to buffer struggles and to enhance celebrations and triumphs. When grown children marry and begin having their own families, the sense of biological kinship becomes renewed by the miracle of grandchildren. The mutual obligations of the flesh are not forgotten.

How foolish it would be to try and run a society that does not respect and cultivate the abiding biological roots of kinship.

My favorite aunt (Lena) passed away April 2008, after a five-year battle with a brain tumor. Mike, her partner/ husband of 46 years had passed approximately four and one-half years prior to her passing. He had succumbed to pneumonia and congestive heart failure. Her daughter, Celeste, and I agreed that like so many lifelong couples, that with his passing, she was ready to go and be with him rather than fight the battle as vigorously as she would have had he been there for motivation. Because of their deep religious convictions, Celeste and I feel that it was easy for her mother to let go of this world and join Mike in a better place. Celeste did admit to some initial hurt...even anger, at her mother's stated desire to pass on to be with Mike, but came to fully understand and accept that her mother's place was with her husband. Lena knew that Celeste had a family of her own and that she would be okay.

As families do, Celeste and her husband moved her mother from her home in Riverside to their place in San Andreas, California, where she lived out her last three years. They provided her with her own place, on their property, where they could take care of her until the end.

I recently received my copy of Lena's memorial DVD. And after viewing it, I was compelled to call Celeste with some personal questions...prompting an in-depth conversation. Our dialogue motivated me to include some final thoughts on my father's youngest sister... Lena.

Mike wasn't Celeste's biological father, but he was the only man that she ever called "Dad." For all practical intents and purposes, he was her father from a very early age. During our conversation I acknowledged that when her mother first started dating Mike, I didn't particularly care for the man...because he was from New York, and it showed. But I later came to agree (with Celeste) that they were meant to be, and that Mike was the best thing that could have happened to her and her mother.

The music was beautiful and perfectly matched to the period and to the person being eulogized. She epitomized the wholesome, girl-next-door look...from Pleasantville. And in every picture of her and Mike (including the ones at his worst, near the end), they always had those loving smiles for each other. It was obvious, even to this skeptic, that theirs was the real thing...they truly loved and cared for each other after all those years.

The caption under Lena's picture, as the DVD began to roll, just struck a chord with me...it read: "Lord have mercy, I'm finally home!"

CHAPTER 19

In the small town of Oakey Oaks, Chicken Little rang the school bell and cried for everyone to "run for their lives!" This sent the whole town into a frenzied panic that caused so much havoc that it destroyed a small part of the town and Oakey Oaks Tower; but eventually everyone calmed down enough to ask him what was wrong, and Chicken Little explained that a piece of the sky, shaped like a stop sign, had fallen on his head while he was sitting under the big Oak tree in the town square. But then he was unable to find the piece. His father, Buck Cluck, ashamedly assumed that this "piece of sky" was just an acorn that had fallen from the tree and hit his son on the head. Chicken Little then becomes the laughing stock of the town.

As a fan of Chicken Little, I've never viewed him as paranoid, but rather as an invigilator of life, who was just ahead of his time...metaphorically speaking of course. But with time and my own maturity, I have come to believe that he probably wasn't a young immature chick, but rather an old-school rooster. Like all departing generations he could see that the incoming generations were out of control, living pin-ball like lives and taking them all to Hell in a hand basket. He was gravely concerned about their direction and the consequences therein. No different than what "we're" seeing and saying today, except that our take is that this group is fast-tracking that snowball rolling downhill to Hell.

There is no questioning that we are living in an accelerated world today, and that the physical and psychological affects are far reaching and yet to be fully understood. I know that I have always been an A-personality, but I also know that trait has intensified over the years. I often joke about needing a "calm me down pill." Every facet of our life is being affected and changed; as Dwight laments in one of those country songs, "And music that I no longer understand."

I would also suggest that our fast, ever-changing world is contributing to our ever-increasing drug problems. I believe that even the younger generations (the ones who actually accept the realities of the real world) are struggling with the rigors of life outside the confines of the family nest. And that's why more and more are still living with, and being subsidized by, their parents. Without the old-school common sense, fortitude and pride, they are ill prepared for today's lifestyle that even they don't always recognize. I joked about my calm me down pill, but I have no doubt that many of today's stressed out, over-extended individuals turn to drugs for their calm me down pills.

We're all touched by addiction, be it drug driven or psychological...and if not directly, then indirectly. We are no longer the anomaly; we are the norm, we just don't talk about the situation. We internalize and hope that our friends and neighbors don't witness the growing financial and emotional erosion of a family in crisis.

Most of you already know that the ravages of drug abuse have profoundly affected my immediate family. Again, it's just my opinion...but I believe drugs offer a haven for those unable to adjust. And once they've experienced that utopian world, they are even less prepared and/or inclined to fight the endless, day-to-day struggles of the real world.

For twenty-something years my son, Landon, has been adrift in a sea of drugs...running from the shadows of his tormenting demons. I was naïve...or in denial about how deeply he had fallen and how truly dark and hopeless his world had become. During our correspondence over the eighteen months he was in prison...the last time, I read letters describing the darkest side of Hell; the unbelievable events that crossed all lines of sanity... stories that shook me to my very core. Landon has met death, face to face, more times than I wanted to know... he has seen the other side (the abode of lost souls). With that knowledge and insight, it is now my hope that he will fight this battle as if it's for his life, because it could very well be. But I fear he is far more comfortable in that other world...

For 25 years our family has endured the emotional highs and lows associated with the chaotic, frustrating and more often than not...heartbreaking task of rescuing one of their own, from the always ebbing and flowing tide of addiction.

Growing up in rural Arkansas, 55 to 60 years ago, drugs...other than alcohol and tobacco, were unheard of. Our current drug epidemic was still festering mainly in the big cities and had not yet begun its tsunami like advance across rural America. But today, the meth-labs are flourishing in our country's heartland, behind the curtains of pristine forest, rolling meadowland and innocuous looking farmhouses sitting back off the road.

While visiting with Jessie one day at his car lot, Howard the "repo-man" dropped by to share a story regarding one of his recent adventures. Jessie introduced us and assured me that I was welcome to stick around and listen to Howard's account of his latest, and always interesting, side-business of repossessing cars and trucks for Jessie and the local banks. Because Jessie carries his own notes on the used cars that he sells, he...like the banks, occasionally calls upon Howard to do the dirty, and sometimes scary work of locating and repossessing said vehicle(s). Although the story was about retrieving a truck for the bank, not Jessie, I stuck around because I thought it might be interesting. But it never occurred to me that it might be book material.

The story goes that the truck was located in the northern part of the state, and just outside the small community of Hatfield, Arkansas. Once there, Howard took a secondary road out of town for several miles before arriving at a county road (gravel) where he turned right. A mile or two down the county road, he then turned onto a narrow, private, dirt road lined on both sides by barbwire fencing. He knew to turn there because the man, back in Hatfield, who gave him the general directions said, "You can't miss the private road turn because there's an old wringer type washing machine sitting there with their mail box attached to the manual wringer's arm."

Howard's wife was riding along with him in case he didn't have time to load the repossession onto his flatbed and they had to make a run for it with each of them driving a vehicle. Yep, I'm already thinking...this doesn't sound good.

So now they're slowly moving down that dirt road that's too narrow to turn that big flatbed around on, even if their situation deteriorated and called for an emergency change of direction. But it gets worse...remember those progressive Burma Shave signs that used to line Route 66, and how they displayed and dispensed information and advice as you traveled along the road? Well...guess what? Yes, as they advanced toward their destination, they were accompanied by signage along both sides of the already constricted lane. They were provided with absolute, matter-of-fact, in your face information and advice...and they (Howard and his wife) didn't have to guess about what the messages were meant to convey. They had somehow entered this real-life Deliverance scenario through some kind of weird time warp. And by now (duh) his wife was expressing her concerns even as Howard (hiding his uneasiness) was trying to reassure her that it would be fine.

The crudely crafted posters read something like this: "If you're not a real American, turn back now before it's too late." "If you're black, you had better have a real good reason for coming down this road." "You still have time to turn around if you don't belong here." "If you're here for the meeting, welcome."

Their persistence landed them in a clearing, in the middle of a wooded area. Howard described the area as very trashy with junk scattered around a couple of rundown trailer houses and numerous vehicles in various conditions...some operational and others obviously inoperable. He also observed what appeared to be some type of construction and/or carpentry work going on near the far side of the clearing. He circled his truck so that he could park it in a heading out (get-a-way) direction. He left his wife behind the steering wheel, with the engine running and the passenger door open on the side facing the front door of the trailer he was about to approach. As he guardedly made his way to the porch area of the dilapidated residence, he not only noticed the truck he was seeking, parked nearby...but was puzzled by the many cases of beer stacked on the front porch... along with an old couch, recliner and a non-functioning refrigerator.

He haltingly knocked on the aluminum entryway and a Bubba-like guy, with a shaved head and multiple tattoos came to the door. He said, "If you're here for the meeting you're way too early, it's not until the weekend." Howard explained that he was just there to repossess that pickup sitting off to the right of the porch. To Howard's surprise, the man just said, "Go ahead and take the son-of-a-bitch, the owner left it here weeks ago. He knew someone would be looking for it and he just wanted to make it more difficult for them to find." He then said, "I'll walk down to the truck with you 'cause I've got some stuff stored in the bed that I need to get out before you take it away."

Howard told us he was still very apprehensive, but was trying to carry on a semi-friendly, kinda joking conversation without appearing to be aware of appearances. He also volunteered that when Bubba first appeared at the door, the opening reeked from an undeniable chemical concoction that permeated even the deck area as Bubba made his way out onto the portico... and he was feeling no pain. Sounds like a meth-lab to me, but the good thing for Howard was that Bubba was high and not in a coming down or crash mode...he would have been ugly and mean in that frame of mind.

Howard also jestingly inquired about all the beer and the construction-like work going on across the yard. He was told, with a straight face, the beer was for the clan's up-coming, weekend recruiting rally and that the carpenters were building crosses.

He didn't bother loading the pickup on his flatbed until he and his wife got back to Hatfield. He just nonchalantly climbed into the truck...but all the while hoping and pleading to the "powers that be" that it would actually start and he could make his get-away. It did, and with his wife already geared-up and ready to go, they were out of there in a flash.

Entirely true, I'm not sure...but I believe the core story is true and represents the realities of life. And that is that everything changes...yet nothing changes.

CHAPTER 20

In spite of the ugliness depicted in the preceding chapter, it was my gut feeling that the racism bandwidth has narrowed substantially in those states that I wandered in and out of on my trips. I'm not throwing this out as a red herring, but as I spoke with various individuals from both sides of the proverbial tracks, the general feedback was that authentic discord rarely reaches the surface in their communities. And I used the word surface because there will always be characters, on either side, who will never completely let go of their subsurface biases...it's human nature. It also felt like the over 40s were the most comfortable with their colorblind society, while the younger populace still seems to keep a subtle distance. I can't help but think it's still a part of their (white and black) engrained lineage...a mind set, a way of life, that's somehow surviving and being passed on from generation to generation (The Lamarckian theory, a theory of biological evolution holding that acquired traits can be inherited). And again, I'm not saying it's right or wrong... just that that's the way it was back then.

But having said all that, I was somewhat surprised when I was advised that I should avoid the Shover Street area after dark. It seems that even Small Town, rural America, now has it's own gang problems.

In speaking with some of the "my age" black guys, I learned that they see some of the same unsettling characteristics in their young males, as I do. But of course I didn't say it; I was just thinking it. The posturing, the baggy pants, the hip-hop jargon and their general "if you diss me, I'll break your face" attitude toward anyone they view as disrespecting them...like they've done anything to deserve respect.

No one likes to hear this because we're all supposed to pretend that there's no real difference between men and women. But there's a politically incorrect fact of life: It takes a man to raise a man. Stick to the truth even when it's not popular...dad (or mentor's) life lesson Number 3.

A boy at birth is an intelligent, tool-using primate with natural instincts of aggression, competitiveness, and yes, violence. We must endeavor to shape, curb and refine those natural instincts and characteristics so that they serve the boy in ways that are positive for him and those around him. And with rare exceptions, what that requires is a father or other strong male role model in his life.

During my formative years there were various men in my Mother's life, but they were neither my father nor father figures...from my perspective. But fortunately, I played high school football and back then (unlike today), the coaches were allowed...even expected, to discipline and build character through hard work and mental toughness...on the field and in the classroom. There were all these rules that made no sense. Running wind sprints until you thought your heart was going to explode, and then being told to run some more because "you were dogging it" (coach's observation). Running those plays and drills over and over again...in that blazing Arkansas heat with humidity levels that almost matched the temperature. Getting caught (by the coaches) coming out of the "picture show" after the weekend, midnight movie (back then, the midnight movie was a big deal). We (three starters) had broken curfew and would pay a price. The following Monday, after an extremely hot and grueling practice, we were instructed to remain on the field as our "curfew obedient" teammates headed for the locker room showers. We had already participated in the usual end of practice, run until you drop wind sprints, but were kept on the field to continue running until we puked...yes, really. We were then encouraged to drink our fill of salt water from the saltwater bucket to replace the salt our bodies had excreted through our sweating. Lesson learned; life is simpler when you plow around the stumps.

And unlike today's school systems and defensive parents, our parents never tried to re-direct the blame. You got in trouble at school...you were in trouble at home. And if it was corporal punishment, you didn't even tell your parents...because they would say you probably deserved it and might even add additional penalties.

I didn't get it at the time, but I came to understand that they (the coaches) weren't trying to make us miserable. They were trying to make us into responsible young men... we as starters, also had an obligation to our teammates. We were expected to lead by example and to be as ready as possible (mentally and physically) for the challenges we would be facing in our upcoming football season.

Their task would not be easy, or accomplished in all cases. A man is honest, fair and just. He will have an honest, not posturing...sense of self-respect. He's self-reliant, and he will accept...and embrace, responsibility for his family. He has humility, grace and respect for others. Above all, he has a sense of humor, especially regarding himself...and a true grasp of real world perspective.

I've often been described as a "man's man," and I have to wonder if those coaches (John Pierce, Wayne Taylor and Leon Turpin) aren't somewhat responsible for the person I became. They seemed to know (even ahead of today's hyper-accelerated world) that if they allowed us to just cruise, we would be accepting mediocre as our norm and that life would sooner or later, leave us behind.

These are some of the thoughts that cross my mind as I read about yet another round of murders in various cities around our country. The violence more often than not seems to occur in our black communities. But before I go any further, allow me to make this clear: Violence within the black community doesn't mean the majority are perpetrators or victims of violence. I'm talking about a group within a group.

Why so many homicides? I think because too many black males aren't black men.

Study after study shows that kids...especially boys, from single-parent households are twice as likely to commit crimes as kids from families where the father is present, regardless of ethnicity. Now look at these numbers: According to the Centers for Disease Control, more than 70 percent of out-of-wedlock births are born to black women. That means you have boys growing up never learning the basics of manhood. Not just in this house or that...but whole neighborhoods.

It wasn't always like this. Before we started killing the black family with kindness through welfare, single parent black households were the exception in this country.

In 1960, single mothers headed just 22 percent of black households...less than the percentage of single parent white households today. By 1970, it was 29 percent. By 1990, it was 40 percent. Today? It's seven out of every 10.

Absent a father in the home, these boys don't have a clue what manhood is about, so they hide behind false, emotional and violent bravado. They think violence is an assertion of manhood. Minor insults become fighting words when one's manhood is faux and fragile. What two men with confidence would let be just an argument becomes a fight. What should have been just a fight becomes a shootout. Inmate logic...be the "baddest" or be on the bottom bunk, so to speak. But real men know that insults come from small people and are not worthy of acknowledgment...another lesson from dad, Number 14, I think.

The numbers from the U.S. Department of Justice don't lie, and you're only fooling yourself if you can't accept that those statistics are a reflection of a growing culture, of false manhood, that has been on the rise in the absence of fathers. Black males commit almost half of all violent crimes, even though they represent just seven percent of the U.S. population. In 2005, homicide victimization rates for blacks were six times higher than the rates for whites, and offending rates for blacks were more than seven times higher than the rates for whites.

That doesn't make it a black thing...nor does it make it a race or poverty thing, it makes it a man thing. But all too often, African-Americans cover their ears when the subject turns to black homicide rates. Yet the fact remains, that nine out of ten times, those deaths are the results of a black hand squeezing the trigger of a gun.

Perhaps the book *Outliers* is the place to start the understanding. Author Malcolm Gladwell revisits the violent feuds of the Appalachian Mountains that resulted in the death of hundreds of men and made the Hatfields and McCoys a part of American lore. Sociologists found that a "culture of honor" was at the root of what seemed only to be a series of misunderstandings and property disputes.

Similarly, I would suggest that a "culture of disrespect" exists among "younger" African-American males... disrespect for authority, disrespect for women and disrespect for one another.

It's almost cliché to point toward the music industry and its glorification of violence to illustrate this truth. Disregard and incivility are as much a part of today's urban music as the T-Pain voice effect. Hip-hop stations support their listeners by offering free gas and school supplies with one hand, while using the other to slap them down with provocative misogynistic lyrics.

And why are some of their community's advocates working for...or associated with, these stations? Shouldn't they be trying to clean up the airways? From my perspective, it just sounds...and looks, like this culture of disregard and/or disrespect is being embraced and perpetuated by a segment of today's incoming, younger, black, male generation(s).

Because of the absence of men (white and black) in so many youngsters' lives today, adults must pay careful attention to interaction between boys, starting in preschool. It's important to teach them early on to respect personal space and to be mindful of when to keep their hands to themselves. Yes, boys will be boys, but smacking a friend in the head today could lead to punching him in the mouth a few years later. And the next time, a gun could be drawn...that is the cold hard reality of our world today.

Profiling...? We can think of profiling in general as a practice where people use an observable or known physical attribute as a proxy or estimator of some other unobservable or unknown attributes. Race or sex profiling is simply the use of race or sex as that estimator. It can also just be a common sense opinion based on historical knowledge and statistics...as in, what are the odds?

The writer believes that even when we are dealt a difficult hand...and unfavorable circumstances come to bear, that ultimately, it's still our story to write.

CHAPTER 21

Ricky Gervais's new film, The Invention of Lying, is about a world where lying doesn't exist, which means that everybody tells the truth, and everybody believes everything everybody else says. "I've always hated you," a man tells a work colleague. "He seems nice, but a bit fat," a woman says about her date. It's all truth, all the time, at whatever the cost. Until one day, when Mark, a down-on-his-luck loser played by Gervais, discovers a thing called "lying" and what it can get him. Within days, Mark is rich, famous, and courting the girl of his dreams. And because nobody knows what "lying" is, he goes on, happily living what has become a complete and utter farce.

It's meant to be funny of course, but it's also a more serious commentary on us all. As Americans, we like to think we value the truth. Time and time again, public-opinion polls show that honesty is among the top five characteristics we want in a leader, friend, or lover; the world is full of woeful stories about the tragic consequences of betrayal. At the same time, deception is all around us. Government officials and public figures are lying to us at a disturbing pace; many of our social relationships are based on little white lies we tell each other. We deceive our children, only to be deceived by them in return. And the average person, says psychologist Robert Feldman... the author of a new book on lying, tells at least three lies in the first 10 minutes of a conversation. "There's always been a lot of lying," says Feldman, whose new book, The Liar in Your Life, came out this month. "But I do think we're seeing a kind of cultural shift where we're lying more, it's easier to lie, and in some ways it's almost more acceptable."

One of Feldman's longtime lying colleagues and the inspiration behind the Fox TV series "Lie To Me," defines a liar as a person who "intends to mislead," "deliberately," without being asked to do so by the target of the lie. Which doesn't mean that all lies are equally toxic, some are simply habitual...as in "My pleasure!" Others might just be altruistic. But each, Feldman argues, is harmful... because of the standard it creates. And the more lies we tell, even if they're little white lies, the more deceptive our society becomes.

We are a culture of liars, to put it bluntly, with deceit so deeply ingrained in our psyches that we hardly even notice we're engaging in it. Spam e-mail, deceptive advertising, the everyday pleasantries we don't really mean..."It's so great to meet you!" "I love your dress!" Have we not become "the omnipresent white noise we've learned to tune out?" Feldman also argues that cheating is more common today than ever. The Josephson Institute, a nonprofit focused on youth ethics, concluded in a 2008 survey of nearly 30,000 high school students, that "cheating in school continues to be rampant, and getting worse." In that same survey, 64 percent of students said they'd cheated on a test during the past year, up from 60 percent in 2006. Another recent survey, by Junior Achievement, revealed that more than a third of teens believe lying, cheating, or plagiarizing can be necessary to succeed, while a brand-new study, commissioned by the publishers of Feldman's book, shows that 18- to 34-year-olds...those of us fully reared in this lying culture, deceive more frequently than the general population.

Teaching us to lie is not the purpose of Feldman's book. His subtitle in fact, is "the way to truthful relationships." But if his book teaches us anything, it's that we should sharpen our skills...and use them with abandon.

Liars get what they want. They avoid punishment, and they win others' affection. Liars make themselves sound smart and savvy, they attain power over those of us who believe them, and they often use their lies to rise up in the professional world. Many liars have fun doing it. And many more take pride in getting away with it.

And then we have the highly evolved fabricators and manipulators who truly understand and work the gullible. Language is at the root of political consciousness. We can only know what we understand, and our understanding is limited by the words and phrases used to frame an issue. The constant repetition of imprecise, politically correct language is sure to have a cumulative effect upon a target audience...eventually we begin to accept what we are told. Indeed, the main goal of political correctness is to diminish the choice of words and thereby reduce the range of thought.

In his book, "The End of Sanity," Martin Gross writes that blatantly irrational behavior is rapidly being established as the norm in almost every area of human endeavor. There seem to be new customs, new rules, new anti-intellectual theories regularly foisted on us from every direction. Underneath, the nation is roiling. Americans know that something without a name is undermining their nation, turning the mind mushy when it comes to separating truth from falsehood and right from wrong.

Orwellian: A word or phrase is considered "Orwellian" when it is impenetrably obtuse or even oxymoronic. The endless blowing of windy rhetoric erodes the objective truth. Reality is then constructed to suit the needs of the moment.

The state of American politics has become increasingly Orwellian. At the national level in particular, career-minded officials who repeat empty and often deliberately misleading or untruthful slogans dominate elected positions. Consider the most recent Presidential campaigns. After reinventing government, we crossed a bridge to the twenty-first century to a place where "no child is left behind," thanks to the wonders of compassionate conservatism. "Change...?" And of course we all remember "Bill's" absurd niggling over what the meaning of "sex" is. Such vacuity strips political communication of any concrete meaning. As this trend continues, our language will ultimately become useless to express the ideas that form the basis of rational political discourse in a healthy republic.

When Arnold Schwarzenegger was running for governor of California (2003), he received counsel from Edward Kennedy. The pearls of wisdom included advice to: "Just don't ever go into details," and "Just always stay 30,000 feet above and talk about your overall vision."

On Kennedy's passing, Schwarzenegger lamented, "Teddy taught us all that public service isn't a hobby or even an occupation, but a way of life."

For me, that's the most compelling statement that I have ever heard in support of term limits. Being a politician should never become a way of life.

The greatest enemy of clear language is insincerity. (George Orwell)

I've come to believe that a cultural war is raging across our country, driven by a generation of media, educators, entertainers, and politicians, in which, with Orwellian fervor, certain acceptable thoughts and verbiage are mandated. And as John Charles Carter (Charlton Heston) expressed so politically correct: "Political correctness" is tyranny with manners.

During his tenure as president of the NRA, Heston spoke from various podiums in defense of our Second Amendment rights...even at a couple of our more liberal colleges.

"You are the best and the brightest. You, here in the fertile cradle of American academia, here in the castle of learning on the Charles River, you are the cream. But I submit that you, and your counterparts across the land, are the most socially conformed and politically silenced generation since Concord Bridge. Before you claim to be a champion of free thought, tell me: Why did political correctness originate on America's campuses? And why do you continue to tolerate it? Why do you, who're supposed to debate ideas, surrender to their suppression? Let's be honest. Who here thinks your professors can say what they really believe? It scares me to death, and should scare you too, that the superstition of political correctness rules the halls of reason."

He then asked for a show of hands from those who owned a gun, and several hands went up. When asked for a show of hands from those who owned more than one gun...a few hands were raised. As he canvassed his audience he announced that he could really care less about who owned what; his concerns were for the gun owners, who in the interest of political correctness, had chosen not to acknowledge their ownership...thereby, psychologically and philosophically giving-up or waving their Second Amendment rights. Caving to political correctness dictated by others.

The Constitution was handed down to guide us by a bunch of wise, middle-aged, white guys who invented our country. But now, many would flinch upon hearing that spoken. Why? It's true...they were white guys. So were most of the guys that died in Lincoln's name opposing slavery in the 1860s. So why should I be ashamed of white guys? Why is Hispanic Pride or Black Pride a good thing, while White Pride conjures up shaven heads and white hoods? Why was the Million Man March on Washington celebrated by many as progress, while the Promise Keepers March on Washington was greeted with suspicion and ridicule? I'll tell you why, Cultural warfare.

If we talk about race, it does not make us a racist. If we see distinctions between the genders, it does not make us a sexist. If we think critically about a denomination, it does not make us anti-religion. If we accept but don't celebrate homosexuality, it does not make us a homophobe.

I would also suggest that those who spent their time and energy, pointing fingers and hurling unfounded accusations of racism, are a part of the problem.

Additionally, I would surmise that it takes one to perceive one.

Hypocrisy is the act of pretending to have beliefs, opinions, virtues, feelings, qualities, or standards that one does not actually have. Hypocrisy is thus a kind of lie. Hypocrisy may come from a desire to hide from others, one's actual motives or feelings.

Watch your thoughts; they become words.

Watch your words; they become actions.

Watch your actions; they become habits.

Watch your habits; they become character.

Watch your character; it becomes your destiny.

"How clever you are, my dear! You never mean a single word you say." (Oscar Wilde)

CHAPTER 22

Each and every one of us entered this world wetting ourselves. We were totally amazed by our multifaceted environment because on a daily basis, everything was new...and challenging. Life often seemed overwhelming with un-winnable hands being dealt in odds-defying numbers. And now, on the way out...too many are leaving just the way they came in...figuratively and/or literally.

There were, of course, times when we just knew we had the world by the tail and that life was going to be a cakewalk. We believed we had all the answers because a few random things had fallen into place...but in most cases, not because of any ingenious or brilliance from our side. I can actually remember thinking that I had reined my life in, and all I had to do from that point on was to keep a tight rein. But we've all heard that old saying, "You don't know what you don't know."

Mankind has always considered itself larger...and smarter than life, and many individuals have even come to view themselves as such. But we were never meant to be all knowing, or masters of the universe. Not only our dynamical system (physical environment), but also the dynamics of human evolution ensures that we'll go out just as baffled as when we came onboard.

It seems that we're willing to fight the battle until at some point, it becomes apparent that it's not only a winless battle, but one without end...and that our only way out is to let go of that "dead hand" and surrender. It's at that juncture that we cash out, step off the express and watch the world leave us behind...and out of touch with reality.

So is it any wonder that today's self-indulgent generations view themselves as having all the answers even as they view their parents and grandparents as out of touch with reality. My guess is that 30- to-40 years from now, the current know-it-alls will be lamenting, "I no longer understand or recognize our world."

Another commonality shared by departing generations is the spiritual acceptance of an "after-life" as their current life winds down. I think most of us have always had that inkling inside, but with our mortality staring us in the face...that notion takes on an elevated sense of urgency. The timing of "losing touch with reality," could also suggest that we've given up on this world and are reaching out to the Promised Land.

Sounds almost hypocritical...waiting until near the end of the game before choosing sides. What were we thinking, that we were immortal and would live forever? Nope! - Just young, dumb, know-it-alls.

That same spirituality also brings clarity to the intangible drivers of this whole *going home* phenomenon.

To *go home* is to experience the peace and love arising from our self-effulgent heart center, the core of our being. We find that all the love and happiness we have ever wanted is already available to us, every moment, without fail.

A deep yearning causes us to search for our innate roots, the womb of our origin. We have gone out into the world, experienced "life" with its pains and pleasures, happiness and sadness. We never found a lasting happiness from those experiences. What we sought was not outside of ourselves.

The outer journey of going away from home to seek happiness was not fruitless. We found irrefutably that the world did not hold a continuous thread of happiness, connecting life's adventures.

The silver thread that weaves its way through life's journeys is our own outlook, realization of being the peace, being the love. What we seek, out in the world, is what we already are in the home of our soul. We are the joy, the peace, and the love. These things are all a part of the makeup of us...just as surely as we could ever imagine. But we have been imagining they are outside in the world, instead of realizing they are at home...in our hearts.

The great experiment, the ultimate goal of our existence, is to find that the qualities that we seek to make us happy are actually already an integral part of our existence. And the way to find these qualities within ourselves is through practice...practicing kindness and caring, practicing meditation, holding positive and unselfish attitudes. Steeped in practice we soon realign with the peace and joy within.

I do not see this line of thought as being at odds with other suppositions that I've already advanced in this book's closing chapter (written some time ago). From the beginning, I've emphasized that "philosophically speaking," there is probably more than one way home; it all depends on one's interpretation of *going home*, and how far (again, philosophically speaking) from home their journey took them.

This morning as I was enjoying my ritualistic cups of coffee, a beautiful monarch butterfly (from out of nowhere) fluttered by my kitchen window. It seemed to hesitate... just for an instant, as if posing symbolically...before disappearing as suddenly as it had arrived. I know that I'm sometimes prone to over analyze, but that butterfly spoke to me...figuratively speaking of course.

In my first book I wrote about the butterfly effect (butterfly theory) and how it can work to alter and/or affect all things, from weather to our personal lives. While I'm not going into a long drawn out explanation regarding the butterfly...or chaos theory, it has provided me with a new line of thought for my writing.

There are few movies where you can palpably sense the presence of the director behind the camera, but this was one of them. The movie is about an old actor who has lost many of those he loves but continues to work. The actor, who at 77 had appeared in 200 movies since 1945, and the director, whose breathing I could almost hear in the background, was 94 and directed his first film in 1931.

As the movie starts and the actor appears, he is onstage in a production of "Exit the King," and the film lingers on speeches in which the old man rails against his mortality and defines the unending memorials which he fancies will keep his name alive. After the play, he learns of a tragic accident that has robbed him of his wife, his daughter and son-in-law. Some time later, we see him living with his young grandson and the nanny.

His offstage life is one of routine, and it is here, with just a touch...both subtle and glancing, that the director makes his most poignant observation about how we die, but life heedlessly goes on without us. Our subject takes his coffee every morning in the same cafe, sitting in the same chair, at the same table and always reading the same local newspaper. As he gets up to go, another man enters, sits at the same table, and unfolds his copy of a different newspaper. This happens day after day.

One morning, the second man arrives early and takes another table. But when his regular table becomes available, he gets up with alacrity to claim it...but is headed off by a stranger who sits down ahead of him. These little scenes had a surprising impact on me. I often think of myself as a regular at places I often visit: That is my restaurant and my table, and when I return there...there is a satisfaction in occupying my table again, because it proves my own continuity. Of course those locations also belong to others, who I will never know, and someday I will never return there, and someday neither will the others, and someday my restaurant will not be there either. Yet daily ritual encourages us to believe that because things have been the same for a long time, they will always be the same.

The old actor sees a handsome pair of shoes in a store window and buys them. For a man past a certain age, to buy new shoes is an act of faith. (One is reminded of the Irish story about the shoe clerk who assured an old man, "These will see you out.") We see the shoes in a close-up as he talks with his agent, a venal man who hints that a young actress might like to meet him.

After all, the agent says, "When Pablo Casals was in his 80s, he married a teenage student." "But I am nowhere near my 80s," he snaps. "And I am not Casals." What eventually happened to those shoes was a reminder that we can make plans but we cannot count on them. There are tender little scenes in which the old man and his grandson play with battery-powered trucks and enjoy each other's company, and fraught scenes in which the agent tries to get the actor to accept a tawdry TV show. And later, a scene from a production of "The Tempest," in which he delivers Prospero's speech beginning with: "Our revels now are ended..."

Few films seem so wise and knowing about the fact of age and the approach of the end. And at his great age, the director dispenses with the silliness of plot mechanics and tells his story in a simple, unadorned fashion...with episodes and observations, trusting us to understand.

In the final scene, as he leaves a cafe without drinking the wine he has ordered, the camera lingers to watch another man walk in and order a beer. And life goes on...

The above just hit home for me; I've never been consciously afraid of dying, but rather a fear of ceasing to exist.

For time is like a fashionable host...it always has two hands held out, one to welcome new guests, the other to say goodbye to departing ones.

CHAPTER 23

A civilized society's first line of defense is not the law, police and courts but customs, traditions and moral values. Behavioral norms, mostly transmitted by example, word of mouth and religious teachings, represent a body of wisdom distilled over the ages through experience and trial and error.

They include important thou-shalt-nots such as shalt not murder, shalt not steal, shalt not lie and cheat, but they also include all those courtesies one might call ladylike and gentlemanly conduct.

The failure to fully transmit values and tradition to subsequent generations represents one of the failings of the so-called greatest generation.

Behavior accepted as the norm today would have been seen as despicable yesteryear. There are television debt relief advertisements that promise to help debtors to pay back only half of what they owe.

To see men sitting whilst a woman or elderly person was standing on a crowded bus or trolley car used to be unacceptable. It was just common decency for a man to give up his seat. Today, in some cities there are ordinances requiring public conveyances to set aside seats posted "Senior Citizen Seating." Laws have replaced common decency.

Profanity...sometimes thinly disguised, sometimes not... is almost unavoidable in advertising, pop culture and in everyday conversation. And there are strong differences of opinion about what constitutes proper dress.

Foul language is spoken by children in front of and sometimes even to teachers and other adults. When I was a youngster, it was inconceivable that foul language would be uttered in the presence of an adult; it would have meant a smack across the face. And...children addressing adults by a first name was unheard of because it was considered disrespectful.

But of course back then, parents and teachers didn't have child-raising "experts" to tell them that "time out" is a means of discipline.

Years ago, a young lady who allowed a guy to have his hand in her rear pocket as they strolled down the street would have been seen as a slut. Today, baby showers are held for unwed mothers. Yesteryear, such an acceptance of illegitimacy would have been unthinkable.

I also know that by this time you're probably tempted to charge, "Richard, you're a prude...an old dinosaur!" Then I would ask you whether high rates of illegitimacy make a positive contribution to a civilized society. If not, how would you propose that illegitimacy be controlled?

In years past, it was controlled through social sanctions like disgrace and shunning.

Years ago, the lowest of low-down men would not say the kind of things often said to or in front of women today. Gentlemanly behavior protected women from coarse behavior. Today, we expect sexual harassment laws to restrain rude or vulgar behavior.

During the 1940s and '50s, my family lived in a small, rural, racially mixed community in Arkansas. Most families never considered locking their doors...and if they did, it wasn't until late at night. Citizens never thought of installing bars on their windows and on many of those hot, humid, summer nights, some of us could be found sleeping outside on the porch swing and/or a pallet made from a homemade quilt.

But starting in the 1960s and '70s things seemed to change...subtle, but change was at our doorsteps. I will only say that our comfort level declined somewhat as folks began securing their families at night. But I would be remiss if I didn't note that our small town changes were, for the most part...innocuous when compared to the big cities around the country.

Keep in mind that the 1940s and '50s were a time of gross racial discrimination, high black poverty and few opportunities compared to today. The fact that black neighborhoods were far more civilized at that time should give pause to the excuses of today that blames today's pathology on poverty and discrimination.

As a replacement for actual human decency and morality, we've turned to political correctness and bloodless legalisms, neither of which is an adequate replacement for doing the right thing...because it's principled or virtuous.

Policemen and laws can never replace customs, traditions and moral values as a means for regulating human behavior. At best, the police and criminal justice system are the last desperate line of defense for a civilized society. Our increased reliance on laws to regulate behavior is a measure of how uncivilized we've become.

Our world has been inalterably changed and we no longer recognize it...and are viewed by today's movers and shakers as archaic. But we have something far more tangible to support our dated position than the opposition has for their know-it-all attitude. We have a different reference point than today's generation (we've witnessed the erosion of society's civility and common sense)...and that's what causes us grief, we can see humanity spinning out of control. What they see today is the norm for them...and because they have no other point of reference, there will be no turning back.

They're just so sure that what they believe is right, just by virtue of the fact they believe it. Traditions? Codes-of-conduct? Religious beliefs? Customs? For them, there's no need to understand why previous generations believed what they did...or to understand what purpose it served. Too many also believe that "we" were all racist back then and so we couldn't possibly have had any good ideas.

Early on in this book I suggested that *going home* isn't about returning to one's physical birthplace or home, but rather to *another time...another place* (*Fridays With Landon*). The truth is that we cannot go home and except for our memories...home, as we knew it, no longer exists. It has been relegated to the archives of a bygone time where we are the keepers and with our passing the past will be lost to the ages. And in time, the reality will be that our era was irrelevant at best, or it was just delusional manifestations of an antiquated, out-of-touch, departing generation.

Or perhaps "the journey" is our home, and the *going home* phenomenon is an innate human need/desire to say good-bye as our journey winds down...as was my farewell tour.

Every journey will eventually realize its intended destination, and it's not important to rush that arrival. Sometimes tossing the map is the best way to get where you really need to go.

But there is yet another applicable country saying: "You can't get there from here."

Random Thoughts:

I felt it was in this book's best, long-term interest to cut it short. I came to realize that I was pushing too hard to populate more and more pages...when the number of pages has nothing to do with the quality of the product. I feel I've reached a point of diminishing returns where I'm throwing things together in an extemporaneous manner and then filling in the gaps with hamburger-helper.

I am becoming increasing impatient with myself, and life in general. I'm also experiencing occasional, unexplainable bouts of anxiety driven by unjustifiable feelings of urgency in regard to day-to-day, mundane tasks and issues. I often question myself; is it just me or is it a subtle, universal symptom of the *going home* manifestation...old age? In my case, it's probably as much about me personally as it is about my age. I'm a prideful (for whatever reason) perfectionist, with an A-personality, and don't want to go out being viewed as a rambling old man that should have left well enough alone...after two books.

Along with my growing puzzlement of life, I'm finding more and more reasons for staying home...only venturing out when necessity dictates, or motivated by friends and/ or family.

From my upstairs computer room (where I do all my writing), a large window provides me with a catbird seat-like-view of a portion of my neighborhood...and the activities and regiments therein. Today, from time to time, I've glanced out at the gardeners performing their weekly routine of trimming, mowing and blowing. I noticed various neighbors coming and going as they attended to their daily tasks of running their lives... their routines. The mail truck just rounded the corner (right on time) and by doing so, alerted me to the fact that I could now, routinely wander on over for my mail. Later, as the kids begin arriving home from school, I can just count on seeing and hearing them at play...while knowing life will routinely replenish itself and continue.

Because I've always been a finisher, closure is important to me as I strive to leave nothing for tomorrow that I can do today. Tomorrow, someone else may be doing things on "my behalf" that I could have done better today. But by the same token, we should always have plans for tomorrow...things to address that will require our presence...a reason to challenge yet another day. Tomorrow is close if we'll just embrace it today..."We cannot think, feel, or act without the perception of some goal."

The above is important to me because I do feel somewhat isolated and/or disengaged from things outside my comfort level, but I believe I'm more the norm than the anomaly...in my age group. Life has given us horizons further than we can see, and without that vision we can only count on today...even as we contemplate and prepare for tomorrow.

I often feel like a ghost...previewing from above, as life plays out below.

From that perspective, I continue to search for a plausible reason that the little house on Harvey Street, where we lived during my early years, is still standing. It was a very modest (even for then) little place sitting somewhere in the middle of a row of about 20-or-so other cookie-cutter look-alikes facing a small highway leading out of town, but "to nowhere that really mattered." Each house had a small gravel driveway leading from the roadway into a singlewide carport, and they came with about a half-acre of land...maybe more, maybe less, behind the structures. At the back edge of those property lines, the railroad had a right-of-way where I spent endless hours fantasizing about being onboard as I watched the smiling faces (like an old black and white, silent movie) flickering passed my location. I was always left with a mesmerizing sadness as that lonesome whistle beckoned even as it was disappearing into the distance. We had the road out front and the train tracks running behind us...yet we never seemed to venture far from our small simple world.

On the first leg of my *going home* journey, I tried (like anyone on this type of journey would) to locate the various landmarks relating to my formative years. I found the physical location of the above referenced house right away, but progress had completely changed the overall makeup of the locality. An interstate highway had cut right through the middle of that row of dwellings. Motels, fast-food eateries, mini-mart service stations, small businesses and some, as of yet, undeveloped vacant lots were skewing my memory of the past. In the center of all this confusion was a single cookie-cutter domicile... standing alone. But without a reference point I had no way of knowing...if this was our house. What were the odds? Well, my guess would be about 20 to 1...give or take.

There was yet another leftover about a half-mile further down that same road (too far to serve as a north star) that stood out conspicuously for me. KXAR had been our radio station...providing local news and announcements, the weather, beef and pork prices, crops and market information, funerals and weddings, the score of the high school's game the night before and even a little rock and roll. The small brick structure was still there... but boarded up, grown over and silent. But unlike the tenants of all those cookie-cutter homes, the progressive staff of KXAR had relocated to its new high-tech facility on Elm Street. In today's world, you progress or progress rolls over you.

I'm bringing this up not only because I love metaphors and symbolism, but also because it has been on my mind since that first foray back there in the spring. I've been wondering if that could actually be the house where I lived, and if so...why was my house the one left standing? Okay, so 20 to 1 odds aren't that bad...could happen.

I had an occasion to visit with Tommy Montgomery while in town and he verified that "yes," that lone little house is in fact, the same house I lived in as a kid. He remembered because he has lived there his entire life...just a mile or so down the road, just past the old radio station.

I see that little house as a symbolical remnant of a departing generation, where most have already given up and stepped back, thereby conceding the struggle. Time is running out and even the holdouts will be discarded as progress and time dictate. The metaphor (from my perspective) is about that old house and me; we began life together, 60-plus years ago...when we were new, shiny and built to persevere. We have both weathered the years and that knowledge gives me cause to reflect on... and remember, a bygone time. It made me feel good to see that my old friend, like myself, was still persisting...and contributing. Like that stout little house, I've endured and held my own longer than most of my contemporaries. Time is a friend to neither of us now, but life's cycles will continue perpetually as life renews.

This should go without saying, but if you're on your way *home*...it's required reading in this case. Most of life's reflective pondering only rises to the conscious level as our remaining time ebbs. I think we become more open to the idea that "perhaps" we were wrong about some of the things that "we just knew" we were right about..."back when." In reevaluating ourselves today, our parameters for that assessment are more tempered...even accepting a grading curve...as in, "I made some mistakes. But I don't need to be reminded...because I haven't forgotten."

"Probably, the greatest source of unhappiness is one's failure to meet the expectations of others."

> Heavenly Father, we come before you today to ask your forgiveness and to seek your direction and guidance.
> We know Your Word says, "Woe to those who call evil good," but that is exactly what we have done.
> We have lost our spiritual equilibrium and reversed our values.
> We have exploited the poor and called it the lottery.
> We have rewarded laziness and called it welfare.
> We have killed our unborn and called it choice.

We have shot abortionists and called it justifiable.
We have neglected to discipline our children and
called it building self-esteem.
We have abused power and called it politics.
We have coveted our neighbor's possessions and
called it ambition.
We have polluted the air with profanity and
pornography and called it freedom of expression.
We have ridiculed the time-honored values of our
forefathers and called it enlightenment.
Search us, Oh God, and know our hearts today;
cleanse us from every sin and set us free.
Amen!

The above prayer has been attributed to Billy Graham
and Paul Harvey.

But it was actually written in 1995 by Bob Russell, who
offered it at the Kentucky Governor's Prayer Breakfast,
in Frankfort.

In 1996, Reverend Joe Wright utilized "his version" of it
as an opening prayer at a session of the Kansas House
of Representatives. It was not well received by a number
of the Democrats.

So what was their problem with the prayer?

The easy answer is that he read a prayer about sin. The
more complicated answer is that Wright jumped into
America's tense debate about whether some things are
always right and some things are always wrong.

When we lose our way, it's not because we lost our sight...
it's because we lost our vision.

Autumn's Road

Days long passed and nights long dark,
Words we thought, but did not impart.
Home is just a word we have known,
For a place we cannot go.

Richard

Going Home

The deception begins in my heart,
Not in the words you say.
I am always fooling myself
Hoping it will be a different way.
Your eyes don't meet mine and
I'm standing on shifting sand.
I reach out to you,
Asking you to take my hand.
But you always turn away
Another brick in your wall.
You've come to the edge of
That bridge again
But can't cross, and finally stall.

So I find myself at crossroads,
Trying to decide which path to take.
One leads to uncertainty, the other
Most surely heartbreak.
Does my heart or my head become the ruler?
Do I travel a road unknown?
And all the while I stand there,
You keep trying to "go home."

But "home" is a destination that
Never truly arrives.
In spite of all the hopes and dreams
And the vast long distance drives.
The mending of tattered moments,
The brushing away of tears,
The assurance of trust and the
Banishing of fears...
It becomes smoke and mirrors,
An illusion of an accomplishment.
But there is no "home,"

Only a place that you rent.

So I find myself at crossroads,
Trying to decide which path to take.
One leads to uncertainty, the other
Most surely heartbreak.
Does my heart or my head become the ruler?
Do I travel a road unknown?
And all the while I stand there,
You keep trying to "go home."

Victoria Dawson

Those were the days...and we thought they would never end.

Mother

Richard Neal

Elvin Neal

Regina Kay Neal

Regina Kay

Elvin and Mother

Regina Kay and Elvin

Richard

Richard McKenzie Neal

About the Author:
Richard McKenzie Neal

One should never equate education and/or intelligence to wisdom...

Richard was born in Hope, Arkansas (Bill Clinton's boyhood home), in 1941 and his father was gone prior to Richard turning two years old. He never knew the man, but attended his funeral as a sixteen-year-old.

Before boarding a Greyhound bus for California, at seventeen, Richard knew two stepfathers and a number of others who were just passing through. During those teen years, before succumbing to the beckoning allure of the outside world, Richard worked at an assortment of low-paying jobs. Summers were spent in the fields... picking cotton and/or watermelons and baling hay. He also worked as a plumber's helper and a carhop at the local drive-in burger stand.

After dropping out of school, eloping and landing in California, he soon realized how far out of his element he had ventured. And without the guidance of his "Constant Companion," Richard would have spent a lifetime floundering in a sea of ignorance and ineptness... and his books would not exist.

Richard's first book (Fridays With Landon) was driven by his son's life-altering heroin addiction. He had hoped not to author a sequel, but left the book open-ended due to historical concerns, which did in fact...resurface. For 25 years the family has endured the emotional highs and lows associated with the chaotic, frustrating and more often than not...heartbreaking task of rescuing one of their own, from the always ebbing and flowing tide of addiction.

The unintended sequel (The Path to Addiction...) was triggered by a mind-numbing relapse after 30 months of sobriety. The second book was then written to bring closure...one-way or the other. The author advanced several possible scenarios for the ending of that book, but only one of those possibilities was favorable...

His third book (The Long Road Home...) is a philosophical journey that we'll all experience as our time here begins to dwindle.

All three books were written after retiring from a very rewarding, thirty-six years in the oil industry.

Our success should be measured by what we gave up (what it cost us) to obtain it...and not by what we accomplished and/or accumulated.

Contributors:

Connie Coats

Gayla Crall

Victoria Davis

Victoria Dawson

Bobby Lee Jones

Lucy Jones

John Smith

Howard Tippitt

Jessie Tullis

Claudia Van Gee

Calvin Ware

www.ingramcontent.com/pod-product-compliance
Lightning Source LLC
Chambersburg PA
CBHW022247290526
45785CB00015B/373